KEY GUIDE
TO AUSTRALIAN
MAMMALS

Spotted Cuscus
Phalanger maculatus

KEY GUIDE
TO AUSTRALIAN
MAMMALS

LEONARD CRONIN

ILLUSTRATED BY

MARION WESTMACOTT

REED

First published in 1991 by
REED BOOKS PTY LTD
3/470 Sydney Road, Balgowlah, NSW 2093

Planned and produced by
LEONARD CRONIN

National Library of Australia
Cataloguing-in-publication data

Cronin, Leonard.
Key Guide to Australian Mammals.

Bibliography.
Includes index.
ISBN 0 7301 03552
1. Mammals—Australia—Identification.
I. Title.

599.0994

Design: Robert Taylor

Additional research: Gertrud Latour

Typeset by Adtype Graphics Pty Ltd
Printed in Singapore through Imago Productions.

CONTENTS

INTRODUCTION

The Australian mammals continue to fascinate and surprise biologists as research gradually reveals more about their adaptations, lifestyles and behaviour. Isolated from the rest of the world for many thousands of years, they have penetrated even the most remote and inhospitable parts of the continent, surviving on the meagre food sources of the arid regions, developing strategies to deal with bush fires, droughts, high summer temperatures and freezing winters. In the past two centuries they have been faced with successive invasions of introduced species, destruction of their habitats and the encroachment of civilisation. Some, like the Grassland Melomys, thrive in association with mankind, reaching pest proportions in sugar cane plantations. Others, like Leadbeater's Possum, retreat to the few remaining patches of old, unlogged forest and watch helplessly as the bulldozers and chainsaws approach.

Over the millenia their strategies for survival have produced such unusual animals as the Platypus, equipped with a sixth sense to detect the minute electrical signals emitted by small aquatic invertebrates; the Marsupial Mole which 'swims' through the desert sands; and the magnificent Red Kangaroo, perfectly adapted to the arid interior with its fast, energy-efficient hopping gait and ability to survive for long periods without drinking.

Australia is the only country where the three types of mammal—marsupials, monotremes and placental mammals—exist side-by-side. While all suckle their young on milk produced in the female's mammary glands they differ in the state of development of their newborn. Monotremes (the platypus and echidna) lay eggs with a leathery shell, while the placental mammals (rodents, bats and marine mammals) give birth to fully-formed young. Marsupials (kangaroos, possums, cuscuses, wombats, koala, bandicoots and the carnivorous marsupials) produce very small, incompletely-developed young. Some marsupials suckle their young in the security of a well-developed pouch, while others offer the newborn little protection, dragging them around while they cling helplessly to the mother's teats.

Most Australian mammals are active during the night and around dawn or dusk. Many live in trees, and some possums have a membrane between the forelimbs and hindlimbs enabling them to glide. Bats have modified limbs with large flight membranes giving them the freedom of the skies, while other mammals have adopted a fast hopping gait, or taken to the water where they use flippers instead of feet.

Australia's hot arid interior supports many mammalian species that hide from the sun by burrowing into the ground. They can survive without drinking by producing highly-concentrated urine and dry faecal pellets, obtaining sufficient free water from their food or by the chemical breakdown of carbohydrates.

Despite this wonderful variety of form and function no comprehensive field guide to the Australian mammals has previously been published. The many thousands of bushwalkers, students and naturalists are faced with the unenviable task of lugging around large heavy volumes and struggling with difficult key systems, or trying to identify a species from memory.

In producing this field guide it has been my aim to help the interested observer to both identify and understand something of the lifestyle of our wildlife. Unlike human beings most Australian animals are shy and cryptic in their habits and do little to modify their environment. Many make their homes in tree hollows, conduct their daily lives under cover of darkness and leave few tracks and traces of their existence. Yet they often have quite complex social systems and remarkable adaptations that allow them to survive in harsh and hostile conditions. Within the limitations of the space available in a field guide I have attempted to give the reader an up-to-date knowledge-base that will satisfy most field requirements and encourage further reading and research.

The information is presented under sub-headings for ease of access. A simple visual key refers the reader to specific pages in the book where positive identification can be made using the illustrations, distribution maps and descriptions. Measurements are intended to give a guide to the relative size of an adult animal, and where possible the animals on a page have been illustrated in proportion to each other. Habitat descriptions indicate the general areas in which the animal is known to live. Many other factors determine their ability to survive, such as appropriate food sources, access to suitable nesting holes in old trees, the type of soil, temperature fluctuations and the presence of other species. The shaded areas on the distribution maps only show where the animal is likely to occur, given an appropriate habitat.

The Latin names used are those currently accepted by the scientific community. However, these may be subject to change as research reveals different affinities, or subspecies are determined to be separate species in their own right. The names of subspecies have been abbreviated to the initial letters of the species followed by the specific name of the subspecies. Thus *Macropus robustus erubescens* is abbreviated to *M. r. erubescens*.

One of the greatest challenges facing the people of Australia is to learn how to coexist with our native wildlife. In our struggle to achieve economic wealth we have failed to consider the requirements of the animals we share this continent with. We destroy their refuges by cutting down ancient forests, then create new habitats with introduced plants and animals. A few native species may proliferate and become pests, but the vast majority disappear altogether or flee to the few remaining natural habitats where they are forced to compete for space and food.

Part of the problem lies in a lack of basic knowledge. The study of our native fauna has never been well-funded, and consequently we know little about the biology and habitat requirements of some of our most common animals. It is interesting to note that this lack of knowledge has been used as a defence by governments, companies and individuals to excuse crimes committed against the environment. Some of these have been far more devastating in their consequences than many crimes committed against society; yet in our justice system the perpetrators of social crimes cannot use ignorance of the law of the land as an acceptable defence.

If we devoted a fraction of the amount of time and money spent on litigation to understanding and upholding the law of nature, we would be able to look forward to a world with a secure future for all our native fauna, rather than watching the list of extinct and endangered species grow longer and longer.

HOW TO USE THIS GUIDE

The following keys have been designed to make the identification of an unknown species as simple as possible. The reader is guided to specific pages in the book where animals fitting the categories described in the keys are grouped together. The boxes in the keys show a single animal or group of animals with similar characteristics. The numbers in the boxes give the pages where these animals are to be found.

The first page of the key describes the monotremes and sea mammals which are quite distinctive and easily categorised. The second and third pages describe the majority of other mammals grouped according to their size. The small mammals are divided into carnivorous marsupials, rodents, possums, potoroo and bettong, rat kangaroo, bandicoots and bilby, and the marsupial mole.

Carnivorous marsupials have a long jaw with a continuous row of teeth. Rodents have a more bulbous jaw and a long gap between the single pair of large upper and lower incisor teeth and the grinding molars. Possums are mostly arboreal marsupials with a long, flexible tail, a quadrupedal gait and usually one or more teeth between the incisors and grinding molar teeth of the lower jaw. The potoroo and bettongs can be distinguished from the bandicoots and bilby by their fast bipedal hopping gait. The bandicoots and bilby have a rather graceless, quadrupedal, galloping run, short tails, pointed faces and coarse, stiff hair.

The last page of the key describes the bats. Examine the head and tail area and compare your animal with the diagrams in the smaller boxes. If it does not correspond to any of these categories, then it will most likely be found in the pages indicated in the large box.

MONOTREMES AND SEA MAMMALS

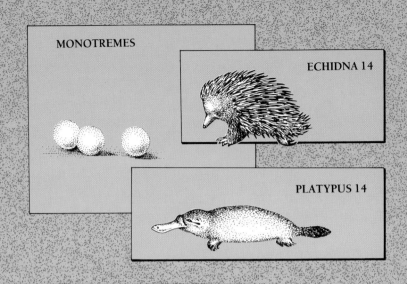

MONOTREMES

ECHIDNA 14

PLATYPUS 14

SEA MAMMALS

SEALS AND SEA-LION 174-178

DOLPHINS AND DUGONG 172-174

HUMPBACK WHALE 178

SMALL MAMMALS

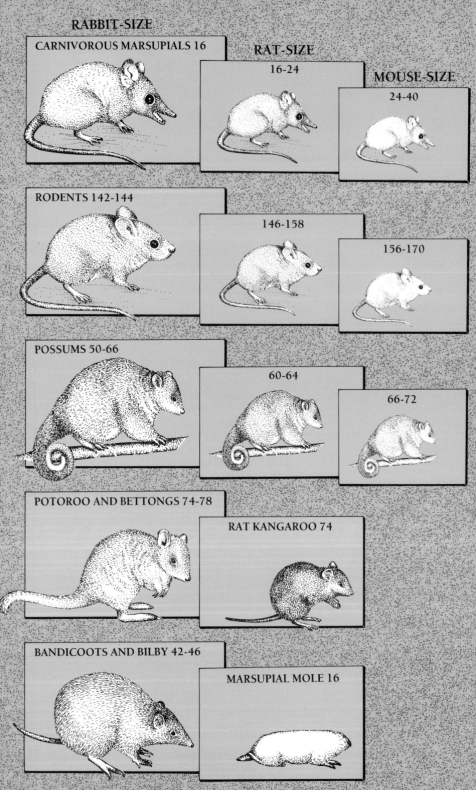

RABBIT-SIZE

CARNIVOROUS MARSUPIALS 16

RAT-SIZE
16-24

MOUSE-SIZE
24-40

RODENTS 142-144

146-158

156-170

POSSUMS 50-66

60-64

66-72

POTOROO AND BETTONGS 74-78

RAT KANGAROO 74

BANDICOOTS AND BILBY 42-46

MARSUPIAL MOLE 16

LARGE MAMMALS

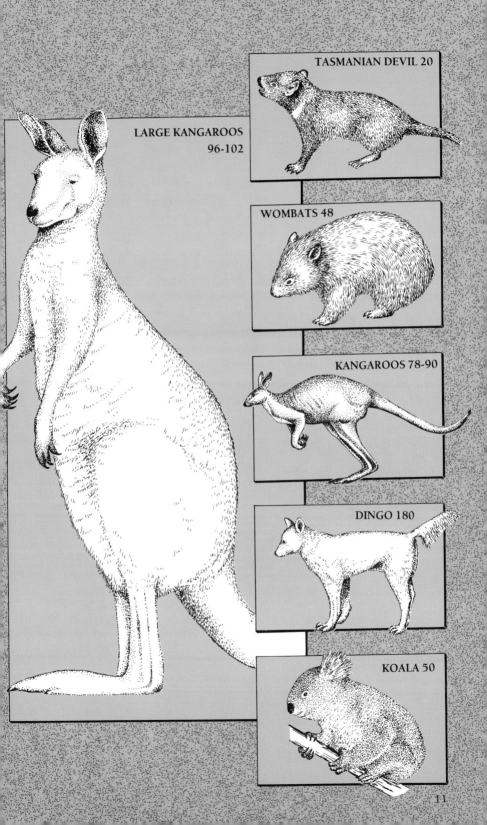

TASMANIAN DEVIL 20

LARGE KANGAROOS
96-102

WOMBATS 48

KANGAROOS 78-90

DINGO 180

KOALA 50

BATS

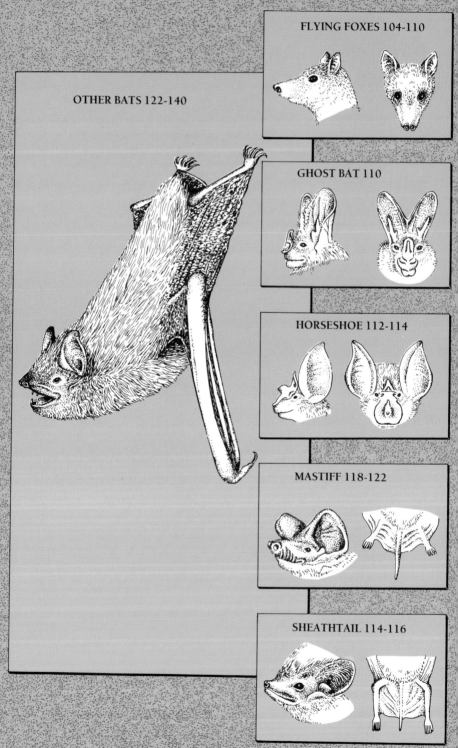

OTHER BATS 122-140

FLYING FOXES 104-110

GHOST BAT 110

HORSESHOE 112-114

MASTIFF 118-122

SHEATHTAIL 114-116

Colour Plates
And
Descriptions

Numbat
Myrmecobius fasciatus

Tachyglossus aculeatus

SHORT-BEAKED ECHIDNA

An egg-laying mammal, the Short-beaked Echidna has stout sharp spines covering the back and sides, a long tubular snout with a long sticky tongue, small eyes and a rudimentary tail. The spines moult annually. They are creamy-coloured with a dark tip, and may be obscured in the Tasmanian form by dark brown to sandy fur. The limbs are short and powerful with five toes and strong spatulate claws. Males have a small non-venomous spur on the hindleg.
Size. Length: 300-450 mm. **Weight:** 2-7 kg. Males are larger.
Behaviour. Active mainly at dawn and dusk in summer and during the day in winter, they sleep under bushes or leaf litter, in hollow logs or abandoned burrows. Usually solitary, they have overlapping home ranges some 800 m across. They have a slow, rolling gait, freezing or curling up if threatened, eventually seeking shelter or burying themselves. They climb onto logs and stumps and dig into termite mounds and ant nests, locating insects by smell and by minute electrical signals detected by receptors in the snout. In cold climates they hibernate for up to 6 months, arousing every 2 weeks or so.
Development. They mate in July and August. Females develop a temporary pouch and lay a single egg, probably directly into the pouch by curling up their abdomen. The egg has a leathery skin, is about 15 mm long and hatches after 10 days. Newborn are blind with very short spines and feed on milk secreted from pores in the pouch area. They are left a hole or burrow for about 3 months when the mother forages, becoming independent at about 8 months.
Food. Termites, ants and other invertebrates gathered by the long tongue.
Habitat. River banks in most habitats from rainforests to deserts.
Status. Common. Also in New Guinea.

Ornithorhynchus anatinus

PLATYPUS

This remarkable, egg-laying aquatic mammal has a streamlined body without external ears, webbed feet, a flattened paddle-like tail, and a rubbery, sensitive, duck-shaped bill. The soft, dense, water-repellent fur is lustrous dark brown on the back, pale cream and sometimes reddish below. The feet have long sharp claws. Males have a sharp hollow spur on the ankles of their hindlegs connected to a venom gland in the groin. Females lose the spur before maturity.
Size. Length: 398-570 mm. **Weight:** 0.67-2.7 kg.
Behaviour. Active from evening to early morning, they sleep in short burrows just above water level, usually with two entrances under tree roots. Breeding females dig a burrow up to 20 m long, plugged at intervals and terminating in a nest chamber lined with grass, leaves or reeds. Solitary and probably territorial, they make a low growl if disturbed, share feeding areas and use several burrows, foraging up to 2 km away, often grooming on a favourite rock or log. They have a waddling walk supported on the knuckles of the hands, and swim smoothly with a rolling dive, closing their eyes, nostrils and ears under water. The bill has receptors on the left side that detect minute electrical signals emitted by aquatic invertebrates. These are sifted from the river bed by the bill, stored in cheek pouches, and chewed and ground between horny ridges after surfacing. They hibernate from May to September in the south.
Development. Females breed at 2 years. Mating takes place in the water from August to October. Two eggs about 17 mm long with soft leathery skins are usually laid in the nest chamber. The mother curls around them until they hatch about 2 weeks later. Newborn feed for 3-4 months on milk secreted from ducts on the mother's abdomen, are weaned at 17 weeks and live to 9 years or more.
Food. Insects, molluscs, worms, other invertebrates and small vertebrates.
Habitat. River banks and lakesides in near-coastal forests and rainforests.
Status. Common. Threatened by human activities.

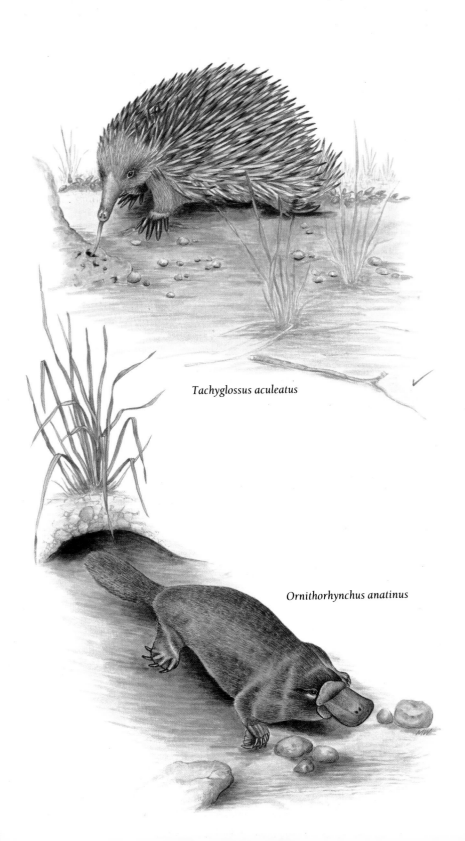

Tachyglossus aculeatus

Ornithorhynchus anatinus

Notoryctes typhlops

MARSUPIAL MOLE

This elusive, unusual animal is adapted to an underground existence. It is blind with tiny vestigial eyes and lacks external ears, having only small holes covered by hair. A horny shield protects the nostrils. The tail is reduced to a leathery stub. The forefeet comprise essentially two spade-like shovelling claws. The hindfeet are clawless. The body is covered with long, silky, golden-brown fur.
Size. Head-body: 120-160 mm. Tail: 20-25 mm.
Weight: 40-70 g.
Behaviour. Little studied, they are probably solitary, living mostly underground, and only occasionally venturing to the surface, particularly after rain. They are extensive burrowers, digging with the forefeet and pushing the soil out with the hindfeet and tail while they progress forward. Burrows are often horizontal, 10-20 cm deep with vertical shafts more than 2 m deep. Tunnels collapse frequently, and in sandy desert soils they seem to swim through the sand. They sleep below ground and may feed on the surface where they pull themselves along in a rapid shuffle, leaving parallel furrows behind and changing direction frequently. They make sharp squeaking sounds if disturbed.
Development. Nothing is known about their development. Females have a deep, rear-opening pouch completely covering two teats. Males do not have a visible scrotum, the testes are located between the skin and wall of the abdomen.
Food. Ants, termites, other insects and their larvae, seeds.
Habitat. Sand dunes and sandy soils of river flats in desert areas.
Status. Common and widespread.

Myrmecobius fasciatus

NUMBAT

The Numbat is the only marsupial adapted to feeding on termites. Like the Echidna it has poorly-developed teeth and a long, sticky, cylindrical tongue that flicks rapidly in and out of the long snout to collect insects. The fur is reddish brown above becoming darker on the rump which has a number of white transverse stripes. The belly is pale grey to white. A dark stripe runs across the eye from ear to mouth. They have a white patch below the eyes and white eyebrows. The ears are large, the tail bushy and flecked with brown and white hairs, the forelimbs have sharp claws.
Size. Head-body: 200-275 mm. Tail: 160-210 mm. **Weight:** 280-550 g.
Behaviour. Active by day, they rest in nests of shredded bark, leaves or other plant material carried in the mouth and placed in hollow logs or at the end of shallow burrows 1-2 m long, using some as refuges and others for overnight shelter. They are solitary with large home ranges of some 100 ha. They have a brisk quadrupedal gait and frequently sniff the air while standing on the hindlegs. They locate termite galleries by scent, digging into the shallow runways leading from the nest.
Development. Sexually mature at about 11 months, they breed from December to March. Up to four young are born some 14 days after mating and attach to the four exposed teats on the mother's abdomen, clinging to hairs surrounding them and being dragged around until furred. They are then left in the nest while the mother forages until they are able to ride on her back, becoming independent at 7 months.
Food. Termites gleaned from logs or shallow galleries. They cannot breach hard termite mounds.
Habitat. Eucalypt forests dominated by Wandoo or Jarrah.
Status. Rare, endangered by fox predation and habitat destruction.

Notoryctes typhlops

Myrmecobius fasciatus

Dasyurus hallucatus

NORTHERN QUOLL

The smallest quoll, this carnivorous marsupial is the size of a large rat. The fur is brownish-grey to brown with white spots on the back, but not on the tail, and cream to white below. The head is long and pointed with large bulging eyes and large pointed ears. The hindfeet have five toes with furrowed pads; the first toe lacks a claw.
Size. Head-body: 120-310 mm. Tail: 125-310 mm.
Weight: 300-950 g. Males are larger than females.
Behaviour. Active mainly at night, they sleep in a hollow log or crevice. They are aggressive, emitting sharp screeches during aggressive encounters. Males and females maintain home ranges. Males may defend an area that includes a number of resident females during the breeding season. Most juvenile males and some females leave the birth area at 6-8 months. They are good climbers although most of their time is spent on the ground.
Development. Sexually mature at 10-11 months, they breed from late June to August with much fighting and many deaths among males. Females have no true pouch although ridges of skin develop on either side of the 6-8 teats during the breeding season. Six young are usually born and remain firmly attached to the teats for 8-10 weeks. They are then left in the den while the mother forages until they are weaned at about 5 months.
Food. Preys upon small mammals, reptiles and insects, also eats soft fruits.
Habitat. Favours rocky areas in open forests, savannah and woodland.
Status. Common.

Dasyurus maculatus

SPOTTED-TAILED QUOLL

A ferocious, cat-sized carnivorous marsupial, the Spotted-tailed Quoll has a powerful body with rich reddish-brown to olive brown fur marked with white spots of various sizes on the back and tail; it is pale creamy-yellow below. The hindfeet have five toes with sharp curved claws and ridged pads. The face is relatively short with a squat, blunt muzzle.
Size. Head-body: 350-760 mm. Tail: 340-420 mm.
Weight: 2-7 kg. Males are larger than females.
Behaviour. Active mainly at night, they sleep in hollow trees or logs, or in rock crevices. On cool winter days they often bask in the sun or forage. Dens are shared by family groups and defended aggressively by both male and female. The male may bring food to the suckling mother. Although mainly terrestrial, they are agile climbers and run with a bounding gait, otherwise their movements are slow and deliberate, sniffing regularly for signs of food. They forage alone, scavenging and hunting opportunistically, killing their prey in a relatively clumsy fashion by biting the back of the neck and head. Males utter growls and staccato cries during courtship, and females make soft 'chh-chh-chh' calls to their young.
Development. Sexually mature at 1 year, they breed from April to August, and copulation may last 8 hours. Females have a shallow rear-opening pouch partially covering six teats. Five young are usually born some 21 days after mating and attach to the teats for about 7 weeks. They are then left in the den while the mother forages, venturing out at 14 weeks, becoming independent at 5 months.
Food. Scavenges dead cattle, sheep and other mammals. Hunts for small mammals, birds, reptiles and insects, manipulating food with the forepaws.
Habitat. Wet and dry sclerophyll forests and rainforests.
Status. Common to sparse. Threatened by logging and competition from feral cats and foxes. Two subspecies: *D. m. gracilis* in northern Queensland; *D. m. maculatus* in southern Queensland and Tasmania.

Dasyurus hallucatus

Dasyurus maculatus

Dasyurus viverrinus

EASTERN QUOLL

The size of a small cat, this carnivorous marsupial is a medium to slender build with dense soft fur. Two distinct colour phases exist, often in the same litter: either black with a brown belly or fawn with a white belly; both have white spots on the back but not on the tail. They have large rounded ears, relatively short legs and only four toes on the hindfeet.

Size. Head-body: 280-450 mm. Tail: 170-280 mm.
Weight: 0.6-2 kg. Males are usually larger than females.
Behaviour. Active mainly at night, they sleep in grass-lined dens in hollow logs, rock crevices or in short burrows. Usually solitary, they have overlapping home ranges, utilising and occasionally sharing a number of dens, particularly during the breeding season when social interactions increase and fighting frequently occurs between males. Males change dens frequently but do not share with other males. Although mostly ground-dwellers they are good climbers, and often stand erect on their hindlegs sniffing the air. They utter a guttural growl when alarmed.
Development. Sexually mature at 1 year, they breed from May to August. Females have no true pouch although ridges of skin develop on either side of the 5-8 teats during the breeding season. More than eight young are usually born, but only those able to attach to a teat survive. They remain firmly attached to the teats and are dragged around by the mother for 6-8 weeks. They are then left in the den or are carried on her back if she changes dens until weaned and independent at 5 months.
Food. They are opportunistic carnivores, scavenging the carcasses of larger animals, and preying on small mammals, birds, insects and worms.
Habitat. Wet and dry sclerophyll forests, heath and scrubland.
Status. Common. The rare Western Quoll (*D. geoffroii*) of arid areas of southwestern W.A., is almost identical, but lacks a fifth toe on the hindfoot.

Sarcophilus harrisii

TASMANIAN DEVIL

Largest of the carnivorous marsupials, the Tasmanian Devil is powerfully built with small eyes set in a short, broad head with strong jaws and well-developed teeth. The fur is black, usually with white patches on the neck and rump. The muzzle and small rounded ears are sparsely-haired. The limbs are short with strong claws.

Size. Head-body: 500-710 mm. Tail: 240-310 mm.
Weight: 4.5-12 kg.
Behaviour. Active mainly at night, they sleep in hollow logs, caves, rock piles or abandoned burrows, following well-defined trails to food sources. They are solitary with large overlapping home ranges of some 10-20 ha, depending on the availability of food, which is often shared with other individuals. In captivity they establish dominance hierarchies and display ritualized aggression including jaw-wrestling and teeth-clashing accompanied by loud growls, yells and screams. Ground-dwellers, they move with an awkward slow lope and a rocking run, and travel many kilometers searching for food.
Development. Females breed from the ages of about 2-6 years and live to about 8 years. They breed from March to early June, giving birth to 2-3 young 31 days after mating. Each attaches to one of the four teats in the mother's backward-opening pouch, where they remain for 13-15 weeks. They are then left in the den while the mother forages, and are weaned at 28-30 weeks.
Food. They are clumsy, inept killers, eating mainly carrion, weak or penned animals such as lambs or poultry, insects and small vertebrates.
Habitat. All habitats, preferring sclerophyll forests, scrub and woodland.
Status. Common.

Dasyurus viverrinus

Sarcophilus harrisii ✓

Dasyuroides byrnei

KOWARI

A rat-size carnivorous marsupial, the Kowari is light grey-brown to sandy-brown above, usually with a darker stripe along the forehead, and greyish-white below. The terminal half of the tail has a brush of dark brown hairs. The pointed head has large eyes and thin, sparsely-haired ears. The limbs are quite long with four toes on the hindfeet.
Size. Head-body: 135-180 mm. Tail: 110-140 mm.
Weight: 70-140 g. Males are larger than females.
Behaviour. Active mainly at night, they are active diggers, constructing or modifying a burrow for daytime shelter from the heat. They sleep in a nest lined with leaves and other vegetable matter, bask in the sun on winter days, and become torpid for short periods when food is scarce. Solitary, they scent-mark a home range with urine and secretions from their chest gland. Vocalisations include a loud defensive staccato chattering and a threatening hiss accompanied by vigorous tail movements. They are ground-dwellers, running with a bounding gait, and sitting up on their hindlegs if disturbed.
Development. Females first breed in their second year, mating from May to December, and copulating for up to 14 hours. They may produce two litters of up to six young per year, born 30-35 days after mating. A shallow pouch forms before birth, leaving the six teats exposed. Newborn attach firmly to the teats and are partially enclosed in the pouch until about 30 days old, when they hang below the mother and are dragged around by her until detaching from the teats some 3 weeks later. They are then left in the nest or cling to the mother's back while she hunts, and are weaned at about 4 months.
Food. Insects, small vertebrates and carrion. They can survive without drinking if their food is moist.
Habitat. Stony deserts with sparse vegetation.
Status. Sparse.

Dasycercus cristicauda

MULGARA

A small, robust, carnivorous marsupial of the sandy Australian deserts, the Mulgara has fine soft fur, light sandy brown with a dark grey base on the back and greyish-white below. The short tail has a fattened, reddish base and a crest of dark brown hairs along the terminal half. The conical head has large eyes and thin, sparsely-haired ears. The hindfeet have five toes with furrowed pads.
Size. Head-body: 125-220 mm. Tail: 70-130 mm.
Weight: 60-170 g. Males are larger than females.
Behaviour. Active mainly at night, they sleep in grass-lined nests in complex burrow systems with several entrances, numerous vertical shafts and deep branching side tunnels, constructed between sand dunes or on the sloping sides of high dunes. They are solitary, socialising briefly during the breeding season, and may be seen basking in the sun on cold days. They run with a bounding gait and sit upright on their hind legs if disturbed. Fast efficient killers, they skin their prey neatly, leaving the inverted skin behind.
Development. Sexually mature at 10-11 months, they probably continue growing throughout their lives, living to 7 years or more. They breed from May to July. Females develop a shallow pouch on either side of their six teats during the breeding season, and give birth to up to six young 35-42 days after mating. Newborn attach firmly to the teats and are dragged around for 55-60 days. They are then left in the nest until weaned at 100-120 days.
Food. Large insects and small vertebrates. They can survive without drinking.
Habitat. Arid, sandy, inland deserts.
Status. Common with scattered, fluctuating populations.

Dasyuroides byrnei

Dasycercus cristicauda

Phascogale calura

RED-TAILED PHASCOGALE

This small carnivorous marsupial is characterised by the colourful tail with reddish-brown fur on the upper surface of the basal third, black fur below and a black, bushy tip. They are ash-grey above and cream to white below, with a pointed face, bulging eyes and large, thin, crinkled ears. The feet and hands have long digits and the feet have a small opposable first toe.

Size. Head-body: 90-125 mm. Tail: 120-145 mm.
Weight: 37-68 g. Males are larger than females.
Behaviour. Little studied, they are known to be predominantly nocturnal, sleeping in tree holes or hollow logs. The are skillful climbers although much of their time is spent searching on the ground for food.
Development. Sexual maturity is reached at about 1 year. Mating takes place in May and June, and up to eight young are born from June to August. The males die soon after mating due to stress-related illnesses. Females have no true pouch although ridges of skin develop on either side of the eight teats during the breeding season. The young attach firmly to the teats and are dragged around by the mother until they relinquish the teat. They are then left in the nest until weaned at 4-5 months.
Food. Insects, small birds and rodents. They can survive without drinking.
Habitat. Eucalypt forests and shrublands with an annual rainfall of 300-600 mm, preferably with a good canopy and numerous nesting hollows.
Status. Common in a restricted habitat. Threatened by logging and introduced predators.

Phascogale tapoatafa

BRUSH-TAILED PHASCOGALE

A predominantly arboreal carnivorous marsupial, the Brush-tailed Phascogale is steel-grey flecked with black above and pale cream below. The tail has a bushy terminal half with black hairs up to 40 mm long, and is not prehensile. The hands and feet have long sharp claws. The first toe of the hindfoot is small and opposes the other four which have very flexible joints enabling them to climb up or down with ease. The forefeet have five long, thin digits. The head is long and pointed with large bulging eyes and long ears.

Size. Head-body: 160-250 mm. Tail: 170-220 mm. **Weight:** 110-235 g. Males are larger than females.
Behaviour. Active mainly at night, they sleep in nests lined with leaves or shredded bark in tree hollows, sometimes shared with several others. Females appear to occupy exclusive home ranges of about 4-5 ha while suckling their young. Males are very competitive during the mating season when their chests become stained with yellow secretions of the chest gland, and die soon after mating due to stress-induced illnesses. They are agile climbers, spending much time clinging head-down below branches. They extract prey from crevices and under bark with their long fingers, and rap their feet on a tree trunk if threatened.
Development. Sexually mature at about 8 months, females may live to 2 years or more. Mating occurs in June, copulation lasts for several hours, and up to eight young are born some 30 days later. Females have no true pouch although ridges of skin develop on either side of the eight teats during the breeding season. The young attach firmly to the teats and are dragged around by the mother for about 54 days. They are then left in the nest until weaned at 4-5 months.
Food. Insects, spiders, centipedes and small vertebrates, caught and manipulated with the forefeet.
Habitat. Open sclerophyll forests with 500-2,000 mm of rain annually.
Status. Common. Subspecies: *P. t. tapoatafa* northern Australia; *P. t. pirata* southern Australia.

Phascogale calura

Phascogale tapoatafa

Parantechinus bilarni

SANDSTONE ANTECHINUS

A mouse-size carnivorous marsupial, the Sandstone Antechinus is flecked greyish-brown above and pale grey below with sandy patches behind the large, thin, crinkled ears. The tail is long and slender, sparsely-haired with visible scales. The head is long with a pointed muzzle almost naked at the sides, and large bulging eyes. The feet have furrowed footpads.

Size. Head-body: 60-100 mm. Tail: 80-115 mm.
Weight: 12-45 g. Males are larger than females.
Behaviour. Little studied, they are known to be mainly active at night, although in the winter they are often seen basking in the sun. They sleep during the day in rock crevices, moving to humid vine thickets in the dry season in search of food. Males are more mobile than females, and the majority of juveniles disperse to a new area. They are agile climbers, although most of the time is spent on the ground foraging for insects.
Development. They reach sexual maturity at one year. Mortality rates are high, and only about one quarter survive to breed twice. The breeding season is from June to August. Four to five young are usually born, each attaching firmly to one of the six teats on the mother's belly. They have no true pouch. The young hang from the mother's teats as she moves around. After detaching from the teats they are left in the nest while the mother forages, and are weaned at 4-5 months.
Food. Insects, larvae and small invertebrates.
Habitat. Rocky escarpments, rugged sandstone country with open eucalypt forests, vine thickets and closed forests.
Status. Common.

Parantechinus macdonnellensis

FAT-TAILED ANTECHINUS

A small carnivorous marsupial of the arid desert regions of Australia, the Fat-tailed Antechinus derives its name from the swollen base of the tail where deposits of fat are laid down when food is plentiful. Poorly-nourished individuals use these fat reserves and consequently have a relatively thin tail. The fur is greyish-brown above and greyish-white below with light reddish-brown patches behind the ears. The head is long with a black-tipped, pointed muzzle, large eyes and ears. The hindfeet are broad.

Size. Head-body: 95-105 mm. Tail: 75-85 mm. **Weight:** 20-45 g.
Behaviour. The behaviour of the Fat-tailed Antechinus has been little studied. They are known to be active mainly at night, sleeping during the day in rocky crevices or in burrows in termite mounds, often emerging during the day in winter to bask in the sun.
Development. Sexual maturity is reached at the age of 10-11 months. They breed once a year in June and July or August and September depending on the region, births being timed to coincide with plentiful food supplies. Females have no true pouch although ridges of skin develop on either side of the six teats during the breeding season, and partially enclose the developing young. Up to six young are born and attach themselves firmly to the teats, where they remain, being dragged around by the mother until they detach and are able to be left in the nest while she forages. Both sexes may survive to breed twice.
Food. Insects and other small invertebrates.
Habitat. Arid rocky hills and desert country.
Status. Common.

Parantechinus bilarni

Parantechinus macdonnellensis

Antechinus stuartii

BROWN ANTECHINUS

A small carnivorous marsupial, the Brown Antechinus is greyish brown above and paler below with a sparsely-haired tail. The head is long with bulging eyes and large, thin, crinkled ears with a notch in the margin. The first toe of the hindfoot opposes the other four.
Size. Head-body: 70-140 mm. Tail: 65-110 mm.
Weight: 17-71 g. Males are larger than females.
Behaviour. Active mainly at night, they usually sleep during the day in a spherical nest constructed of plant material in a hollow log or crevice. On cold days they huddle together in communal nests and bask in the sun during the day; becoming torpid for a few hours to conserve energy when food is scarce. They have a home range of up to about 1 ha. Males have a scent gland on the chest that enlarges during the mating season. They are aggressive and establish dominance hierarchies, the strongest securing better habitats and mating priority. All adult males die from stress-related illnesses soon after mating.
Development. Sexually mature at about 10 months, females may live for up to 3 years. Mating takes place in August in the south and September in the north. Copulation lasts about 6 hours, and up to 10 young are born 26-35 days later. Females have no true pouch. Ridges of skin develop on either side of the 6-10 teats before birth. The young remain firmly attached to the teats for 40-45 days and are dragged around by the mother until they detach and are left in the nest while she forages. They make excursions from the nest at about 75 days and are weaned at 3 months.
Food. Cockroaches, beetles, spiders and other small invertebrates.
Habitat. A variety of forest habitats to 1,600 m including rainforests, wet and dry sclerophyll forests and pine plantations.
Status. Common and abundant.

Antechinus flavipes

YELLOW-FOOTED ANTECHINUS

A small carnivorous marsupial, this colourful antechinus has a slate grey head grading to orange-brown on the sides, belly, rump and feet, white patches on the throat and belly, a pale ring around the eye and a black tail tip. Northern animals are more brightly coloured. The head is long and pointed with a black muzzle tip, bulging eyes and thin, crinkled ears. The hindfeet are very broad.
Size. Head-body: 85-165 mm. Tail: 65-155 mm.
Weight: 21-80 g. Males are larger than females.
Behaviour. Active mainly at night, they sleep in a roughly constructed nest lined with leaves and other vegetation in hollow logs, rocky crevices, caves or buildings. They move quickly and erratically and can run upside down along branches, gripping with their broad feet. They pounce on their prey, killing quickly and efficiently with bites to the head and neck, leaving the skin of small mammals turned inside-out. They utter high-pitched squeaks if threatened. Males die from stress-related illnesses soon after mating.
Development. Sexually mature at 10-11 months, they mate in August in the north and September in the south, copulating for as long as 12 hours. Up to 12 young are born some 30 days after mating, although only eight survive to attach to the eight teats on the mother's abdomen. Females have no true pouch. Ridges of skin develop on either side of the teats 2 weeks before birth. The young detach from the teats at about 40 days. They are then left in the nest or ride on the mother's back while she forages, and are weaned at 3 months.
Food. Insects, with small vertebrates, flowers and nectar.
Habitat. Rainforests, wet and dry sclerophyll forests to dry mulga woodlands.
Status. Common and abundant.

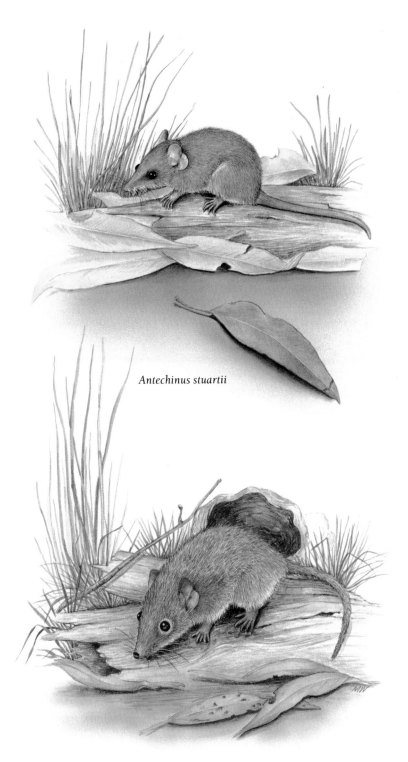

Antechinus stuartii

Antechinus flavipes

Sminthopsis murina

COMMON DUNNART

A small carnivorous marsupial, the Common Dunnart is similar in appearance and habits to the Ooldea Dunnart (*S. ooldea*) of arid central Australia. The fur is slate grey above and white below. The head is long and pointed with bulging eyes, large ears and a slender muzzle. The hindfeet are less than 3 mm wide with a very small first toe. The tail is slender, sparsely-haired with visible scales.
Size. Head-body: 64-105 mm. Tail: 68-100 mm.
Weight: 16-28 g. Males are larger than females.
Behaviour. Little studied, they are known to be active mainly at night, sleeping during in cup-shaped nests 70-100 mm wide of dried grass and leaves constructed in hollow logs, grassy tussocks, natural crevices or grass-trees. Males are very aggressive during the mating season, often fighting over females who attract them by a repetitive chit-chit-chit call.
Development. They breed from August to January, giving birth to two litters of 8-10 young each season, born only 11-14 days after mating. Newborn attach firmly to the mother's 8-10 teats and are completely enclosed in a well-developed circular pouch with a central opening. They develop rapidly, vacating the pouch at about 34 days, and are left in the nest while the mother forages. They are weaned at about 65 days and reach adult size at about 150 days. The pouch regresses after weaning.
Food. Spiders, beetles, caterpillars, cockroaches, small lizards and mice.
Habitat. Woodland, open forest and heathland with an annual rainfall above 250 mm.
Status. Common.

Antechinus swainsonii

DUSKY ANTECHINUS

A small, stocky carnivorous marsupial, the Dusky Antechinus has soft, dense fur, deep chocolate-brown to blackish-brown above and pale grey below. The head has a long pointed muzzle, small eyes and ears. The hindfeet are broad with the first toe opposing the other four; the forefeet have long curved claws for digging.
Size. Head-body: 90-190 mm. Tail: 75-130 mm.
Weight: 35-180 g. Males are larger than females.
Behaviour. Active both day and night, they sleep in shallow burrows often dug into creek banks or under logs. Less than 1 m long, they terminate in a spherical, grass-lined nest chamber about 100 mm across. Females may use several burrows, moving their young if disturbed. Generally solitary, males are very aggressive in the mating season and all adult males die of stress-related illnesses within 3 weeks of mating. Very active and fast-moving, they are often seen climbing among the lower limbs of trees, digging and searching among leaf litter for food.
Development. Sexually mature at about 11 months, they mate in June or July (September in Tasmania and the Snowy Mountains). Copulation is violent and may last 6 hours. Up to 10 young are born 28-35 days later, but only those able to attach to the mother's 6-8 teats survive. Females have no true pouch, ridges of skin enlarge around the teats before birth, forming a shallow pouch divided by a central ridge. The young remain firmly attached to the teats for 33-43 days and are dragged around for 33-43 days. They are then left in the nest, making excursions from the nest at about 75 days. They are weaned at 3 months.
Food. Worms, insects, lizards and other small animals. Prey is captured and manipulated with the forepaws.
Habitat. Wet sclerophyll forests with a dense understorey, rainforests and alpine heaths.
Status. Common. Subspecies: *A. s. swainsonii* Tasmania; *A. s. mimetes* mainland Australia.

Sminthopsis murina

Antechinus swainsonii

Sminthopsis leucopus   WHITE-FOOTED DUNNART

A mouse-size, slightly-built carnivorous marsupial, the White-footed
Dunnart has soft, light grey fur on the back, becoming darker
on the rump and pale-grey to white below. The tail is scaly
with sparse, coarse hairs. The hindfeet are very narrow
with furrowed pads. The head has a long pointed
muzzle, large bulging eyes and large rounded ears.
Size. Head-body: 65-120 mm. Tail: 45-105 mm.
Weight: 7-41 g. Males are larger than females.
Behaviour. Active mainly at night, they usually sleep
during the day in roughly-shredded bark nests in tree hollows,
rotting logs, wood piles and other dry, protected sites. They are
solitary. Females have small discrete home ranges and usually travel no more than
about 80 m to find food, males have overlapping home ranges and may travel up to
1 km for food. They are very fast on the ground and probably good climbers.
Development. Little is known about their development. The breeding season
extends from July to October and females may produce two litters of 8-10 young
per season. Newborn attach firmly to the mother's 8-10 teats and are completely
enclosed in a circular pouch with a central opening.
Food. Insects and their larvae, small reptiles and possibly small mammals.
Habitat. Woodlands and open forests with good ground cover, heathland,
sedgeland, tussock grassland and coastal scrub.
Status. Common. Subspecies: *S. l. leucopus* Tasmania; *S. l. ferruginifrons* mainland
Australia.

Sminthopsis virginiae   RED-CHEEKED DUNNART

A small carnivorous marsupial of northern Australia and New
Guinea, the Red-cheeked Dunnart has short, spiky fur,
blackish-brown flecked with white above, white, yellow or
rufous below, with reddish cheeks and a distinct blackish
stripe down the forehead. The tail is narrow, sparsely-
haired and scaly. The hindfeet are narrow with four long
toes and a small first digit. The head is long and
pointed with large bulging eyes and large rounded ears.
Size. Head-body: 80-126 mm. Tail: 85-135 mm. **Weight**: 15-80 g.
Behaviour. Little is known about their behaviour. They are active
mainly at night, sleeping during the day under logs. Females build a
shallow, saucer-shaped nest of shredded leaves and grass shortly before the young
are born. They are solitary except during the mating season.
Development. The breeding season extends from October to May. Females may
produce two litters per season of up to eight young (six in New Guinea). They are
born 20-22 days after mating, attach firmly to the mother's eight teats (six in New
Guinea), and are fully-enclosed in a well-developed circular pouch with a central
opening. When they emerge from the pouch the young are left in the nest while the
mother forages for food.
Food. Insects, spiders and possibly small vertebrates.
Habitat. Tropical woodlands and swampy savannah.
Status. Common in limited habitats. Australian subspecies: *S. v. virginiae*
northeastern Qld; *S. v. nitela* N. T. and the Kimberleys.

Sminthopsis leucopus

Sminthopsis virginiae

Sminthopsis crassicaudata   FAT-TAILED DUNNART

A widespread, mouse-sized, carnivorous marsupial, the Fat-tailed Dunnart is brownish-grey above and light grey to white below. The fur has a dark base and sandy-grey tips. The tail is short with a fat base in well-nourished individuals, and tapers to a point. The head is pointed with bulging eyes and very large ears.
Size. Head-body: 60-90 mm. Tail: 40-70 mm.
Weight: 10-20 g.
Behaviour. Active only at night, they sleep during the day in nests of dried grass or other plant material constructed beneath logs, rocky crevices or fissures in the cracked soil in arid areas. Groups of individuals often huddle together in a nest in cold conditions to keep warm. They become torpid for a number of hours if the food supply is short, dropping their body temperature to conserve energy and utilising fat reserves in the tail. They are generally solitary with large unstable home ranges that change according to the food supply.
Development. Sexual maturity is reached at 4-5 months, although females do not breed in the year of their birth. The breeding season extends from June to February with two birth peaks in August and September, coinciding with the seasonal abundance of food. The gestation period is very short, 8-10 young are born only 13 days after mating. They attach firmly to the 8-10 teats in a well-developed circular pouch with a central opening. They detach from the teats at 43 days and leave the pouch permanently at about 60 days. They are then left in the nest while the mother forages until they are weaned at about 70 days.
Food. Insects and other small invertebrates. They can exist without drinking if the food is moist.
Habitat. Moist coastal to arid inland areas with open woodlands, low shrubland, tussock grasslands or gibber plains.
Status. Common.

Sminthopsis granulipes   WHITE-TAILED DUNNART

A small, delicate, carnivorous marsupial, the White-tailed Dunnart, although common in its habitat, has been little studied. The fur is quite long and soft, with a blue-grey base and dark brown tips on the back, giving an overall light fawn to grey colour. The tail is white with a thin dark brown stripe along the upper surface. The head is pointed with a narrow muzzle, large bulging eyes and large ears with a notched margin.
Size. Head-body: 69-88 mm. Tail: 56-66 mm. **Weight:** 18-37 g.
Development. The breeding season is probably between May and July. Females have a circular pouch with a central opening.
Food. Insects and their larvae, spiders and centipedes.
Habitat. Low shrubland, sparse mallee with shrubby ground cover, mostly on sand.
Status. Common.

Sminthopsis crassicaudata

Sminthopsis granulipes

Sminthopsis hirtipes

HAIRY-FOOTED DUNNART

A small, mouse-size, carnivorous marsupial of the drier regions, the Hairy-footed Dunnart has been little-studied, partly because of the unsuccessful collecting techniques used. The fur is yellowish-brown to grey-brown above and light grey to white below. The base of the tail is slightly swollen. The feet are unusual, being broad and long (16-19 mm) with fat digits covered with fine silvery hairs forming a fringe around the sole. The hairs are thought to help them walk on soft sand. The head is long with a narrow pointed muzzle, large ears and large bulging eyes.
Size. Head-body: 70-85 mm. Tail: 75-95 mm. **Weight**: 14-20 g.
Development. Little is known about their development. Lactating females have been found in February and April, suggesting a summer breeding season, although it is likely that the breeding season relates to rainfall with population increases after sufficient rain. Females have six teats enclosed in a circular pouch with a central opening.
Food. Insects and their larvae.
Habitat. Sandy arid to semi-arid low open woodlands, shrublands and hummock grasslands.
Status. Common although sparsely scattered.

Sminthopsis macroura

STRIPE-FACED DUNNART

This small, widespread, carnivorous marsupial is found over vast areas of the arid and semi-arid regions of Australia. The fur is brownish-grey to dark brown flecked with light grey above, with a prominent dark strip along the forehead, and pale grey to white below. The head is long and pointed with large bulging eyes and large ears. The tail is long, sparsely-haired with a fattened base in well-nourished individuals, and tapers to a point.
Size. Head-body: 70-100 mm. Tail: 80-110 mm. **Weight**: 15-25 g.
Behaviour. Little studied, they are active mainly at night, sleeping during the day under rocks or logs, or in cracks in the ground. When the food supply is short they enter a state of torpor for a few hours, lowering their body temperature to that of the surroundings, conserving energy and using the fat stored in the tail.
Development. Sexual maturity is reached at 4-5 months in females and about 8 months in males. The breeding season extends from July to February. Two litters of 1-8 young are usually produced each year. The young are born only 12.5 days after mating and firmly attach to the eight teats in the mother's well-developed, centrally-opening, circular pouch. They detach from the teats and leave the pouch at about 40 days and are left in the nest while the mother forages until they are weaned at about 70 days.
Food. Insects and other small invertebrates. They may be able to exist without drinking, obtaining sufficient water from their food, and producing very concentrated urine.
Habitat. Arid and semi-arid low shrubland, woodland and tussock grassland.
Status. Sparse, widespread. Subspecies: *S. m. macroura* central eastern Australia; *S. m. froggatti* central Australia; *S. m. monticola* Blue Mountains.

Sminthopsis hirtipes

Sminthopsis macroura

Planigale gilesi

PAUCIDENT PLANIGALE

A tiny desert-dwelling carnivorous marsupial, the Paucident Planigale has soft, dense fur, cinnamon-grey with a black base above and olive-buff below. The head is flattened and triangular with small rounded ears and protruding eyes. The tail tapers to the tip and may be flattened for most of its length, sometimes with faint dark bands. The limbs are short with five toes and granular pads on the digits. Unlike other planigales they have only two premolar teeth.
Size. Head-body: 44-85 mm. Tail: 48-72 mm. **Weight:** 4-16 g.
Behaviour. Active mainly at night, they sleep in nests in hollow logs, under bark, or in short burrows sometimes with a number of side tunnels and sleeping chambers. In winter they may share nests for warmth, bask in the sun, and become torpid for short periods when food is scarce. They occupy shifting home ranges of some 2,000 square metres, and are very mobile for most of the year, travelling 1 km or more during the night. They become more sedentary during the breeding season when the females stay in small home ranges. Males may establish dominance hierarchies. Vocalisations include an aggressive 'chh-chh' or 'ca-ca', a high-pitched twittering when afraid, and a clicking sound during courtship. They walk moving the hindfeet outside the body line, keeping low to the ground, with a scurrying run and short leaps and bounds. They are good climbers and swimmers.
Development. They breed from August to February. Copulation may last more than 2 hours, and females can produce two litters per season. Six to eight young are usually born 16 days after mating, each attaching firmly to one of the 12 teats in the mother's rear-opening pouch, where they remain for about 37 days. Thereafter they are suckled in the nest until 65-70 days old.
Food. Insects, small mammals and lizards. They are ferocious hunters and efficient killers, killing animals as large as themselves.
Habitat. Sandplains, floodplains and creek beds with cracked clay soil when dry and cover of woodlands, grasslands or sedges.
Status. Sparse with seasonal population fluctuations.

Antechinomys laniger

KULTARR

This mouse-size carnivorous marsupial of the arid and semi-arid regions is fawn-grey to sandy brown above and white below, with a dark ring around the eye and a darker forehead. The tail is very long and thin with a bushy tip of darker hairs. The head is large with bulging eyes and very large ears. The hind legs are very long with only four toes.
Size. Head-body: 70-100 mm. Tail: 100-150 mm.
Weight: 20-40 g
Behaviour. Active mainly at night, they sleep under logs, rocks, grass tussocks, in cracks in the soil, in the burrows of other small animals; or they may dig shallow burrows, concealing the entrance with grass. They are generally solitary, coming together during the mating season. They have a bounding gait, changing direction rapidly to escape predators, and stand up on their hind legs if disturbed or inquisitive.
Development. Sexually mature at 8 months, they breed from July to February. Females may produce more than one litter of usually five young per season. The young each attach to one of the mother's six or eight teats, and are partially enclosed in the rear-opening pouch for about 48 days. They are then left in the nest or ride on the mother's back while she forages for food, becoming independent at about 3 months.
Food. Insects and other small invertebrates.
Habitat. Desert plains, arid and semi-arid grassland and scrubland.
Status. Rare, scattered. Subspecies: *A. l. laniger* eastern Australia; *A. l. spenceri* central and western Australia.

Planigale gilesi

Antechinomys laniger

Planigale tenuirostris
NARROW-NOSED PLANIGALE

This tiny carnivorous marsupial derives its name from the slender flattened snout used to probe into cracks or litter in search of prey. The silky fur has a black base with brown tips giving the back a russet-brown appearance flecked with black, and a faint dark stripe down the forehead. The belly is olive-buff to white. The ears are large with a number of folds. The tail is short and thin.
Size. Head-body: 44-75 mm. Tail: 40-72 mm.
Weight: 3-10 g.
Behaviour. Active mainly at night, they sleep in nests in hollow logs, beneath bark, in grass clumps or short burrows sometimes with a number of side tunnels and sleeping chambers. In winter they may share nests for warmth, bask in the sun, and become torpid for short periods if food is scarce. They have shifting home ranges and may travel more than 500 m in one night. Males have larger home ranges and travel widely during the breeding season, probably searching for females to mate with, fighting frequently and scent-marking areas with their chest gland. Males may establish dominance hierarchies in which the largest have mating preferences. Vocalisations are often loud and include an aggressive 'chh-chh-chh', a defensive 'ca-ca-ca' and high-pitched twittering when stressed. They are agile climbers, and have a scurrying gait with the legs moving alongside the body. They often stand upright sniffing the air and eat sitting up, manipulating food with the paws.
Development. Little studied, they breed from August to February, producing more than one litter of 6-8 young per season. Newborn each attach firmly to one of the 10-12 teats in the mother's rear-opening pouch.
Food. Spiders, beetles, grasshoppers, cockroaches and other insects. They are ferocious hunters, killing insects as large as themselves.
Habitat. Sandplains, floodplains and creek beds with cracked clay soil when dry and cover of woodlands, grasslands or sedges.
Status. Sparse with seasonal population fluctuations.

Planigale maculata
COMMON PLANIGALE

A small, ferocious, carnivorous marsupial, the Common Planigale is cinnamon to grey-brown above, sometimes flecked with white, pale brown to white below with a white chin. The head is triangular and flattened with small eyes and large ears with notched margins. The thin tail is shorter than the head and body.
Size. Head-body: 65-100 mm. Tail: 51-95 mm. **Weight:** 6-22 g.
Behaviour. Active mainly at night, they sleep alone or with others in saucer-shaped nests lined with grass and shredded bark in crevices, hollow logs, beneath bark or under rocks. They bask in the sun on cold days and become torpid for short periods when food is scarce. In the breeding season males fight frequently and scent-mark with their chest gland, probably establishing dominance hierarchies which give the largest mating preferences. They are adept climbers and freeze if disturbed.
Development. Sexually mature at about 10 months, both sexes may breed for at least 2 years. The breeding season extends from October to January in the east with peaks in spring and summer, and lasts all year in the Northern Territory with several litters per year. Females have 8-13 teats in a rear-opening pouch, and give birth to 5-15 young about 20 days after mating. Newborn attach firmly to the teats for about 21 days, vacating the pouch at 45 days, and remaining in the nest until weaned at about 70 days.
Food. Insects and small vertebrates, some as large as themselves.
Habitat. Wet areas with cover of trees, shrubs, sedges or grass.
Status. Common. Subspecies: *P. m. maculata* on the mainland; *P. m. sinualis* on Groote Eylandt.

Planigale tenuirostris

Planigale maculata

Macrotis lagotis

BILBY

A delicately-built rabbit-size marsupial of the desert regions, the Bilby has long, soft, silky fur, bluish-grey on the back, sandy-brown on the flanks and the end of the muzzle, whitish below and on the tip of the tail. The rest of the tail is black with a crest of hairs. The narrow head has large rabbit-like ears, a long pointed snout and a long slender tongue. The short forelimbs have no first digit, the others are long with strong curved claws. The hindfeet are long with a very large strongly-clawed fourth toe, the second and third toes are fused with a double claw.
Size. Head-body: 290-550 mm. Tail: 200-290 mm. **Weight:** 0.8-2.5 kg. Males are much larger than females.
Behaviour. Strictly nocturnal, they are active mainly after midnight, sleeping in burrows up to 2 m deep and 3 m long spiraling steeply down, often with side tunnels and separate entrances in termite mounds, grass tussocks or below shrubs. Adult males have a number of exclusive burrows scent-marked by their anal glands, sometimes shared with one or more females and their young. A rigid dominance hierarchy is established among males without fighting; females have their own less rigid hierarchy and utter sharp growls in aggressive encounters. They have home ranges up to 14 ha, shifting according to the food supply. Their vision is poor, their hearing and sense of smell acute. They often stand upright sniffing the air and run with a cantering gait with the tail held stiffly aloft, waving like a flag.
Development. Breeding mainly from March to May, they mate in the burrow and give birth to 1-3 young after a pregnancy of 21 days. Females have eight teats in a rear-opening pouch. Newborn attach firmly to the teats, vacate the pouch at 70-75 days, and are weaned some 14 days later.
Food. Termites, ants, larvae, seeds, bulbs, fruit and fungi obtained by digging into the soil. They can survive without drinking.
Habitat. Arid and semi-arid shrublands, spinifex and tussock grasslands.
Status. Sparse to rare. Endangered by introduced predators and habitat destruction.
Subspecies: *M. l. lagotis* Warburton Range, W.A.; *M. l. sagitta* central Australia.

Echymipera rufescens

RUFOUS SPINY BANDICOOT

Found also in the rainforests of New Guinea, this rabbit-size marsupial has coarse, stiff fur, rufous-brown flecked witn black and grey above, becoming blacker on the shoulders and head, straw-coloured to white below. The tail is short, black and almost naked. The head is long and narrow with small eyes, small rounded ears and a long tapering snout with a naked tip. The short forelimbs have strong curved claws on elongated feet. The hindfeet are long with a very large, strongly-clawed fourth toe; the second and third toes are fused with a double claw.
Size. Head-body: 300-400 mm. Tail: 75-100 mm. **Weight:** 0.45-2 kg. Males are larger than females.
Behaviour. Little studied, they are nocturnal and strictly terrestrial, moving with a slow hop and a galloping run. They use their forefeet to dig conical holes in the search for food, and investigate the hole with the snout.
Development. Little is known about their development. They breed in February. Females have a well-developed rear-opening pouch with four teats.
Food. Insects, possibly small rodents, fruit and soft tubers.
Habitat. Tropical rainforest, open forests, woodlands and adjoining heath.
Status. Common.

Macrotis lagotis

Echymipera rufescens

Perameles gunnii

EASTERN BARRED BANDICOOT

This slender, graceful, rabbit-size marsupial is conspicuously marked with 3-4 pale bars on each side of the rump. The fur is soft and dense with prominent coarse guard hairs, mottled greyish-fawn above, paler on the flanks and pale grey to white below. The short pointed tail is white above with a dark base. The elongated head has large pointed ears and small eyes. The short forelimbs have strong curved claws on long feet. The hindfeet are long with a very large, strongly-clawed fourth toe; the second and third toes are fused with a double claw used for grooming.
Size. Head-body: 270-400 mm. Tail: 70-110 mm. **Weight:** 0.45-1.2 kg.
Behaviour. Strictly nocturnal, they sleep in domed nests over shallow depressions usually in dense undergrowth. Solitary, they use several nests and rabbit burrows for temporary shelter. Males have overlapping home ranges of about 25 ha; those of females average 3 ha. When alarmed they stand upright sniffing the air, and run with an agile galloping or bounding gait with leaps up to 1 m. Food is located by digging conical holes with the forefeet and probing with the snout. Vocalisations include snuffles, squeaks, hisses and grunts.
Development. Sexually mature at 3-4 months, they live to 3 years or more, breeding from winter to early autumn with a peak from July to November. Females raise 3-4 litters of usually 2-3 young per year. Born only 12.5 days after mating, they attach to some of the eight teats in the mother's rear-opening pouch, which they vacate after 48-53 days. They are then left in the nest while the mother forages until they are weaned at about 60 days.
Food. Insects, larvae, worms and berries. They can survive without drinking.
Habitat. Savannah woodlands and grasslands.
Status. Common in Tasmania, confined to a small area on the mainland.

Isoodon obesulus

SOUTHERN BROWN BANDICOOT

This solidly-built rabbit-size marsupial has soft underfur and coarse bristly guard hairs. The back is brownish-grey flecked with yellow-brown and the belly creamy-white. The tail is short with a pointed tip, the head long and tapering with a naked nose, small rounded ears and small eyes. The short forelimbs have strong curved claws on elongated feet. The hindfeet are long with a very large, strongly-clawed fourth toe; the second and third toes are fused with a double claw used for grooming.
Size. Head-body: 275-360 mm. Tail: 90-140 mm. **Weight:** 0.4-1.6 kg.
Behaviour. Nocturnal, they sleep in a nest of heaped vegetation with a hollow centre, concealed in a depression among ground litter or dense vegetation. Solitary and aggressive, their survival depends on the establishment of an adequate home range. Male home ranges may be up to 7 ha, those of females about 2 ha. Males range widely over areas inhabited by several females, only interacting to mate. They have a moderately fast agile galloping gait, and walk quadrupedally. Food is located by digging conical holes with the forefeet and probing with the snout. Squeaky grunts are made during aggressive encounters.
Development. Sexually mature at 3-4 months, they may live to 3 years or more. They breed from winter to the end of summer, producing 2-3 litters per year. Up to six young are born and attach to some of the eight teats in the mother's rear-opening pouch, becoming independent at 60-70 days.
Food. Insects and their larvae, worms, berries and small vertebrates.
Habitat. Dry sclerophyll forests, grasslands, heathlands, scrub and regenerating areas with good ground cover.
Status. Common with a patchy distribution due to land clearing.

Perameles gunnii

Isoodon obesulus

Perameles nasuta

LONG-NOSED BANDICOOT

The size of a rabbit, the Long-nosed Bandicoot is often seen in suburban gardens. The fur is greyish-brown flecked with dark brown above, creamy-white below and white on the feet. The tail is short and pointed, the head long with a slender muzzle and relatively long pointed ears. The short forelimbs have strong curved claws on elongated feet. The hindfeet are long with a large strongly-clawed fourth toe; the second and third toes are fused with a double claw used for grooming.

Size. Head-body: 310-475 mm. Tail: 120-195 mm. **Weight:** 0.85-1.1 kg.

Behaviour. Nocturnal, they sleep in well-concealed nests of ground litter piled over shallow depressions, with a hollow centre, loose entrance and sometimes with soil kicked over the top for waterproofing. Rabbit burrows are occasionally used, and males and females may share a nest. Males establish dominance hierarchies and both sexes occupy home ranges. They move moderately fast with a galloping gait and walk quadrupedally. Food is found by digging conical holes with the forefeet and probing with the snout.

Development. Sexually mature at 4-5 months, they breed at any time with a lull from late autumn to mid-winter. They rear several litters of usually 2-3 young per year, born only 12.5 days after mating. Newborn attach to some of the eight teats in the mother's rear-opening pouch, which they vacate at about 50 days, remaining in the nest until weaned at about 2 months.

Food. Insects, larvae, worms and plant roots.

Habitat. Rainforests, wet and dry sclerophyll forests and woodlands.

Status. Common. Subspecies: *P. n. nasuta* south of Townsville; *P. n. pallescens* north of Townsville.

Isoodon macrourus

NORTHERN BROWN BANDICOOT

Often found in suburban gardens, this rabbit-size marsupial is dark brown above flecked with light brown, and pale grey to white below. The elongated head has relatively small pointed ears and small eyes. The tail is short and pointed. The forelimbs have strong curved claws on long feet. The hindfeet are long with a very large, strongly-clawed fourth toe; the second and third toes are fused with a double claw used for grooming.

Size. Head-body: 300-470 mm. Tail: 80-215 mm. **Weight:** 0.5-3.1 kg. Males are larger than females.

Behaviour. Nocturnal, they sleep in concealed nests of ground litter piled over shallow depressions, with a hollow centre, loose entrance and exit, and soil kicked over the top for waterproofing. They use several nests, and may shelter in hollow logs and grass tussocks. Solitary, the males are aggressive, marking areas with a scent gland behind the ear and occupying home ranges of about 5 ha; female home ranges are about 2 ha. They run with an agile galloping gait and walk quadrupedally. They locate food by smell, digging conical holes with the forefeet and probing with the snout.

Development. Sexually mature at 3-4 months, they live to 3 years, breeding throughout the year in the north, in winter spring and summer in the south. Females rear several litters of 2-4 young per year, born only 12.5 days after mating. They have eight teats in a rear-opening pouch to which the young attach for about 50 days, remaining in the nest until weaned at 2 months.

Food. Insects, larvae, worms, berries, grass seeds and plant roots.

Habitat. Woodlands, forests and grasslands with low ground cover.

Status. Common. Subspecies: *I. m. macrourus* W.A. and the N.T.; *I. m. torosus* eastern Australia. Also in New Guinea.

Perameles nasuta

Isoodon macrourus

Lasiorhinus latifrons

SOUTHERN HAIRY-NOSED WOMBAT

Distinguished from the Common Wombat (*V. ursinus*) by its silky
fur, hairy nose and slightly smaller size, this large marsupial
is grey to brownish-grey above and paler below. The ears
are narrow and pointed, the eyes small and the head
broad and flattened. The tail is very short and hidden
by fur. The limbs are short with short toes bearing
stout flattened claws; the first toe of the hindfoot
is very small; the second and third toes are fused with
a double claw used for grooming.
Size. Head-body: 770-940 mm. Tail: 25-60 mm. **Weight**: 19-32 kg.
Behaviour. Active mainly at night, they bask in the sun on winter
days, sleeping in deep humid burrows to conserve energy and water. The entrances
are clustered to form a large central warren with smaller warrens surrounding it,
occupying an area 200-300 m across. Each warren system is occupied by 5-10
wombats. Males generally stay in the central warren and females move between
warrens. Males become aggressive during the breeding season. Usually slow and
clumsy, they can run at up to 40 kph if necessary.
Development. Sexually mature at 3 years, they live for more than 20 years in
captivity. The breeding season extends from late September to December, although
they do not breed in drought conditions. Usually a single young is born and
attaches to one of the two teats in the mother's rear-opening pouch, emerging 6-9
months later, and following the mother until weaned at 1 year.
Food. Grasses and herbs. They can survive for long periods without drinking.
Habitat. Arid and semi-arid woodlands and shrublands.
Status. Common in a limited habitat.

Vombatus ursinus

COMMON WOMBAT

A large squat marsupial, the Common Wombat has long, coarse
fur, patchy brownish-grey or dull sandy-brown above and
paler below. The head is broad and large with a flattened
naked nose, small eyes and small hairy ears. The tail
is very short and hidden by fur. The limbs are short
with short toes bearing stout flattened claws. The
first toe of the hindfoot is very small; the second
and third toes are fused with a double claw.
Size. Head-body: 850-1150 mm. Tail: 20-30 mm.
Weight: 22-39 kg.
Behaviour. Solitary and aggressive, Wombats are mainly nocturnal,
foraging during the day in winter. They sleep in burrows up to 20 m long, often
with several entrances and nesting chambers with underground connecting tunnels,
usually dug in slopes above creeks and gullies. Shorter burrows 2-5 m long are used
for temporary shelter. Burrows are dug in a common area and some are shared. If
the ground is too hard they use caves and hollow logs for shelter. Individuals use
more than 10 burrows, visiting 1-4 burrows each night and alternating between
three major sleeping burrows. They move slowly and clumsily within overlapping
home ranges of 5-23 ha. Individuals scent-mark and defend feeding sites.
Development. Sexually mature at 2 years, they breed at any time of the year on the
mainland and in winter in Tasmania. A single young is usually born and attaches to
one of the two teats in the mother's rear-opening pouch, where it remains for about
5 months, following the mother until weaned at about 17 months. Wombats live to
5 years in the wild and 20 years in captivity.
Food. Graze on native grasses, herbs and roots.
Habitat. Forested areas with nearby grassy sites, scrub and heath.
Status. Common. Subspecies: *V. u. ursinus* Flinders Island; *V. u. hirsutus*
southeastern mainland; *V. u. tasmaniensis* Tasmania.

Lasiorhinus latifrons

Vombatus ursinus

Petropseudes dahli

ROCK RINGTAIL POSSUM

A rabbit-sized marsupial, the Rock Ringtail Possum has long woolly fur, grey to brownish-grey above with a dark stripe from forehead to rump, white below with white patches around the eye and under the ear. The short tail is thick at the base and tapers to a thin, nearly naked terminal half. The head is pointed with a naked nose and small rounded ears. The legs are short with short claws on hands and feet. The first two fingers of the forefeet oppose the other three. The hindfeet have an opposing first toe; the second and third are fused with a double claw.
Size. Head-body: 320-390 mm. Tail: 200-266 mm. **Weight:** 1.2-2 kg.
Behaviour. Active at night, they rest in rock clefts and fissures. They are not known to build nests, and are usually seen in pairs or family groups, touching each other frequently, congregating in groups of up to nine on or near rocks. They are shy and run for cover when caught in a spotlight, using a quadrupedal gait. The least arboreal of the ringtails, they are nevertheless good climbers and leapers, and sit on their tail when resting.
Development. Little is known of their breeding biology. They are thought to breed all year, giving birth to a single young that attaches to one of two teats in the mother's forward-opening pouch and rides on her back when older.
Food. Leaves, flowers and fruits of trees and shrubs.
Habitat. Rocky escarpments and outcrops with deep fissures in open forest and vine forest thickets.
Status. Common in appropriate habitats.

Phascolarctos cinereus

KOALA

This short and stocky marsupial has fine woolly fur, light to dark grey above with brown and white patches, and white to yellowish below. The head is broad and flat with large hairy ears, a naked flattened nose and small eyes. The tail is reduced to a stump. The limbs are long with long pointed claws. The first two fingers of the forefeet oppose the other three. The hindfeet have an opposing first toe, the second and third toes are fused with a double claw.
Size. Head-body: 680-820 mm. **Weight:** 7-13.5 kg. Males are larger than females. Northern animals are smaller with shorter fur.
Behaviour. Active mainly at night, they are usually seen resting or feeding in the upper branches of eucalypt trees. Solitary, they will sometimes attack other koalas in their home range (up to 240 m wide). Males use secretions of their chest gland to mark a territory which may overlap that of a female. Juveniles disperse to find their own home range at about 2 years old, becoming nomadic if no suitable area is available. They climb slowly, grasping a tree trunk with the forefeet and pulling the hindlimbs up. They can jump up to 2 m between branches. On the ground they walk quadrupedally, run with a bounding gait, and can swim if necessary. Their vocal repertoire includes bellowing, high pitched yelps, soft grunts, snarls, wails and screams.
Development. Koalas mate in trees, giving birth to a single young (rarely two) from October to March, 34-36 days later. Newborn attach to one of two teats in the rear-opening pouch, which they vacate at 6-7 months, and ride on the mother's back until weaned at 1 year. Females are sexually mature at 2 years, males at 3-4 years, and live to 15 years, although most survive only 3-4 years.
Food. Eucalypt leaves. They can survive without drinking in winter.
Habitat. Eucalypt forests and woodlands.
Status. Common. Threatened by land clearing.

Petropseudes dahli

Phascolarctos cinereus

Pseudocheirus herbertensis

HERBERT RIVER RINGTAIL POSSUM

The northern and southern races of this arboreal marsupial are distinguished by their colour. The former are pale fawn above with a dark stripe along the head and a creamy white belly. Southern animals are dark brown to black above and white below, usually with a white eye ring and white-tipped tail. They have a long pointed face, small rounded ears, bulging eyes and a narrow, tapering, prehensile tail carried in a coil. The first two fingers of the forefeet oppose the other three. The hindfeet have an opposing first toe, the second and third are fused with a double claw.
Size. Head-body: 300-380 mm. Tail: 325-395 mm. **Weight**: 0.7-1.5 kg.
Behaviour. Active at night, they sleep in tree hollows, fern clumps or dense vegetation, sometimes making spherical nests using shredded bark or other vegetation. Solitary, they are agile, cautious climbers, making small, careful leaps through the canopy. On the ground they walk quadrupedally. Vocalisations consist of quiet clicks, grunts and screeches.
Development. They mate from April to December with a peak in May-June, usually producing one litter of twins each year. Newborn attach to the two developed teats in the forward-opening pouch, which they vacate at 115-120 days. They ride on the mother's back for 2 weeks, and are left in the nest until weaned at 150-160 days.
Food. Leaves, flowers and fruits.
Habitat. Rainforest above 300 m and occasionally tall open eucalypt forest.
Status. Sparse. Subspecies: *P. h. hebertensis* from Ingham to Kuranda; and *P. h. cinereus* between Mt Malloy and Bloomfield.

Pseudocheirus peregrinus

COMMON RINGTAIL POSSUM

Often seen in suburban gardens, this rabbit-size marsupial has a variable grey to almost black back sometimes tinged with rufous, and is white to bright rufous below, with pale patches below the ears and eyes, and rufous-tinged legs. The long, white-tipped prehensile tail has a fat base and tapers to a slender tip with a friction pad below. It is carried in a coil when not used. The ears are small and rounded. The hands are grasping with two digits opposing the other three. The hindfeet have an opposing first toe, the second and third are fused with a double claw.
Size. Head-body: 300-390 mm. Tail: 300-390 mm. **Weight**: 660-1100 g.
Behaviour. Active at night, they rest in spherical nests (300-350 mm diameter) in tree hollows, dense undergrowth, the forks of tree trunks or shrubs. Nests have a circular entrance and are lined with shredded bark or grass carried in the curled tail. Male and female pairs often build and use a number of nests, sometimes in the same tree. They have overlapping home ranges and juveniles are forced to disperse. They emit soft, high-pitched twittering calls and secrete a strong-smelling liquid from their anal glands when handled. Almost exclusively arboreal, they are agile climbers and good leapers. On the ground they move quadrupedally, and can swim well.
Development. Sexually mature at about 13 months, they may live to 5 years or more. Twins are usually born from late April to November, and two litters a year may be raised. Newborn each attach to one of the four teats in the mother's forward-opening pouch for 42-49 days, vacating the pouch at 125-130 days. Juveniles remain in the nest or are carried on the mother's back while she forages until they are weaned at 180-210 days.
Food. Mainly eucalypt leaves, also flowers and fruits.
Habitat. Forests, woodlands, rainforests, tea tree thickets, dense shrublands and suburban gardens.
Status. Common and widespread.

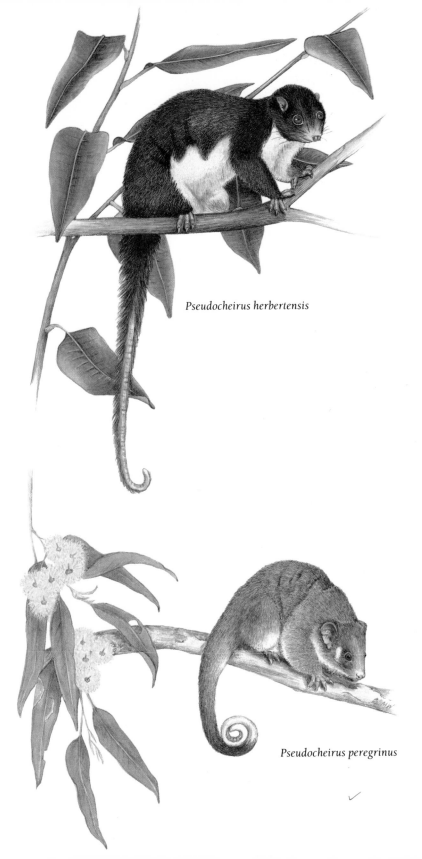

Pseudocheirus herbertensis

Pseudocheirus peregrinus

Hemibelideus lemuroides

This predominantly arboreal marsupial is usually seen high in the forest canopy. The fur is soft, uniformly dark charcoal-grey above, sometimes brownish on the shoulders and lighter below with a yellowish tinge. The face is short with a roman nose and small ears. The eyes shine brilliant silvery-yellow at night. The long prehensile tail is bushy, slightly tapered with a short, naked, finger-like tip, coiled when not used. The hands are grasping with the first two digits opposing the other three. The hindfeet have an opposing first toe, the second and third toes are fused to form a single digit with two claws.
Size. Head-body: 310-350 mm. Tail: 335-375 mm. **Weight**: 0.8-1.3 kg.
Behaviour. Strictly nocturnal, they are quite gregarious, often seen in pairs or family groups, and may feed in the same tree with other groups or individuals. Family groups may share a den located in a tree hollow. They are noisy animals, frequently leaping 2-3 m through the canopy with their legs outstretched like a glider and crashing into the foliage. They occasionally emit loud screams and wails and produce a musky-smelling, sticky, creamy-coloured secretion from their anal glands when handled. On the ground they move quadrupedally.
Development. Little is known about their development. They breed from June to November, producing a single young that attaches to one of two teats in the well-developed forward-opening pouch. The young ride on the back of the mother after emerging from the pouch.
Food. They feed mainly on leaves, supplemented by flowers and fruits.
Habitat. Upland tropical rainforest above 450 m.
Status. Sparse in a limited habitat. Threatened by clearing of rainforests.

Pseudochirops archeri

This rabbit-sized arboreal marsupial has thick soft fur, greyish green to lime-green above with two silvery-yellow stripes from the shoulders to the rump on each side of the spine, and is white below with white patches around the eyes and ears. The pointed head has a pink nose, bulging eyes and small rounded ears. The relatively short prehensile tail has a thick base and tapers to a narrow tip that is curled up when not used. The first two digits of the forefeet oppose the other three. The hindfeet have an opposing first toe; the second and third are fused with a double claw.
Size. Head-body: 340-380 mm. Tail: 310-330 mm. **Weight**: 1.1-1.4 kg.
Behaviour. Active mainly at night, they sometimes feed during the day, and sleep upright on an exposed branch curled into a tight ball with the tail between the hindlegs and coiled under the chin. Most of their active time is spent in the canopy where they can move with surprising speed and agility, although they avoid leaping. On the ground they move quadrupedally. The Green Ringtail Possum is perhaps the most solitary of the ringtails; only occasionally are they seen in pairs, probably when mating or when accompanied by their young.
Development. Sexually mature at about 12 months, they probably breed all year with a peak from July to November, giving birth to a single young that attaches to one of two teats in the mother's forward-opening pouch. The young ride on the mother's back after vacating the pouch..
Food. Leaves, preferably of fig trees.
Habitat. Dense upland tropical rainforest above 300 m.
Status. Sparse in a limited habitat. Threatened by clearing of rainforest.

Hemibelideus lemuroides

Pseudochirops archeri

Phalanger orientalis GREY CUSCUS

The Grey Cuscus is a relatively lightly-built arboreal marsupial of the northern rainforests. The soft woolly fur is grey-brown above and off-white below. A brown stripe extends from the ears to the rump. Males have a distinct yellowish chest gland and a yellow tinge on the side of the neck. The bare skin is greyish-brown. They have a triangular head with bulging, forward-facing eyes that shine red at night, and small, round, projecting ears. The terminal two-thirds of the long prehensile tail is naked with a rough undersurface. The feet have strong curved claws and the first two toes of the forefeet oppose the other three. They have long canine teeth.

Size. Head-body: 350-400 mm. Tail: 280-350 mm. **Weight:** 1.5-2.2 kg.
Behaviour. Cryptic and solitary, they sleep in tree hollows during the day and climb slowly and deliberately through the canopy at night searching for food, gripping branches with the digits of their forefeet and using the tail as a fifth limb. On the ground they move with a slow bounding gait. Males are probably territorial, using their chest gland to scent-mark areas. Vocalisations include harsh aggressive guttural screeches, grunts and clicks.
Development. Little is known about their development. They probably breed throughout the year, usually giving birth to twins that attach to two of the four teats in the mother's forward-opening, well-developed pouch. Infants are carried on the mother's back after vacating the pouch. Males grow throughout their life.
Food. Mainly herbivorous, they eat leaves, fruits, flowers, buds and seeds.
Habitat. Rainforests and some woodlands.
Status. Sparse. Also in Timor, Ceram, New Guinea and the Solomons.

Phalanger maculatus SPOTTED CUSCUS

An arboreal marsupial of the northern rainforests, the Spotted Cuscus is heavily-built with a very short snout and a flat round face with large, forward-pointing, red-rimmed eyes. The dense woolly fur is grey above and creamy-white below and hides the small ears. Males have irregular creamy-white spots on the back, females are more uniformly grey, usually with a white rump. The bare skin is yellowish-pink. The long, strongly prehensile tail is naked for the terminal two-thirds with a rough undersurface, and is coiled up tightly when not in use. The feet have strong curved claws and the first two toes of the forefeet oppose the other three. They have long canine teeth.

Size. Head-body: 350-440 mm. Tail: 315-430 mm. **Weight:** 1.5-3.6 kg.
Behaviour. Active mainly at night and on cool, overcast days, they are usually seen alone, resting on exposed branches in clumps of foliage, or sleeping on small temporary platforms of leaves pulled under themselves. Males are territorial and aggressively defend an area defined by scent-marking. They climb slowly and deliberate through the canopy without leaping, holding branches in a vice-like grip with the feet and using the tail as a fifth limb. On the ground they move with a bounding gait. Vocalisations include guttural screeches and grunts.
Development. Little is known about their development. They probably breed throughout the year, usually giving birth to 1-2 young that attach to some of the four teats in the mother's forward-opening, well-developed pouch. Infants are carried on the mother's back after vacating the pouch.
Food. Omnivorous, they eat leaves, fruits, insects, small birds and mammals.
Habitat. Mainly rainforests to 820 m, some open forests and mangroves.
Status. Sparse. Abundant in New Guinea.

Phalanger orientalis

Phalanger maculatus

Wyulda squamicaudata

SCALY-TAILED POSSUM

A rabbit-size arboreal marsupial and the only member of the genus, the Scaly-tailed Possum has pale grey fur on the back with a slightly darker stripe running from the crown to the rump. It is creamy-white below and sometimes rufous around the base of the prehensile tail, which is naked for most of its length with prominent scales. The head is quite long with a flattened pink nose, small ears and large bulging eyes. The hindfeet have an opposing first toe, the second and third are fused with a double claw.

Size. Head-body: 290-400 mm. Tail: 255-350 mm. **Weight:** 1.25-1.85 kg.
Behaviour. Active at night, the Scaly-tailed Possum sleeps by day in a rock crevice or deep within a rock pile. They are solitary, with a home range some 250 m wide. Active on the ground and in trees, they are agile climbers, using the prehensile tail as a fifth limb.
Development. The breeding season extends from March to August. The single young remains in the mother's forward-opening pouch for 147-151 days, and is weaned at about 35 weeks. Females are sexually mature at about 2 years, males at 18 months.
Food. Leaves, blossom, fruits, seeds and insects.
Habitat. Open and closed forests and vine thickets in rugged, rocky terrain with more than 900 mm of rain annually.
Status. Rare to common in a limited habitat.

Trichosurus caninus

MOUNTAIN BRUSHTAIL POSSUM

A relatively large and robust arboreal marsupial, the Mountain Brushtail Possum is a flecked steel-grey above and whitish below with a black, bushy, curved, tapering tail with a naked undersurface at the tip. Animals in the northeastern part of the range are dark grey to deep amber-brown above. The ears are short and rounded and the nose is pink. The hands have five non-opposing fingers. The hindfeet have an opposing first toe, the second and third are fused with a double claw.

Size. Head-body: 400-570 mm. Tail: 340-420 mm. **Weight:** 2.2-4.5 kg.
Behaviour. Active mainly at night, they sleep in tree hollows, logs or sometimes among epiphytes. Both sexes maintain overlapping home ranges some 500 m wide. These are marked with secretions of scent glands located under the chin, on the chest and below the base of the tail. They are generally solitary, although some pairing seems to occur, probably during the mating season. Juveniles remain in the mother's home range until 2-3 years old. They move rapidly through the trees using the moderately prehensile tail, often crashing through the canopy, and frequently descending to the ground to feed. They can also swim competently if necessary. Usually relatively quiet and docile, they emit guttural snorts when disturbed, and freeze in a spotlight.
Development. The breeding season extends from March to June. A single young is born 15-17 days after conception. It attaches to one of two teats in the mother's forward-facing pouch, which it vacates 5-6 months later, and then rides on the mother's back until weaned at 7-13 months. Males are sexually mature at 30-36 months, females at 2-3 years. Males live to about 12 years, females to about 17 years.
Food. Leaves, fruits, fungi, lichen, bark and pine cones.
Habitat. Wet sclerophyll forests, rainforests and moist gullies.
Status. Common.

Wyulda squamicaudata

Trichosurus caninus

Trichosurus vulpecula

COMMON BRUSHTAIL POSSUM

This rabbit-size arboreal marsupial is silver-grey above and off-white to cream below, although it may be black in southern areas or coppery-coloured with a rufous belly in rainforest habitats. The tail is bushy with a naked area beneath the tip, black, relatively short and moderately prehensile. The ears are large and pointed. There are dark patches on the muzzle and white patches below the ears. The hindfeet have an opposing first toe, the second and third are fused with a double claw.
Size. Head-body: 350-550 mm. Tail: 250-400 mm. **Weight:** 1.5-4.0 kg. Tasmanian animals are larger and more woolly.
Behaviour. Nocturnal, they rest in tree hollows, logs, dense undergrowth, rabbit holes and roof spaces. Individuals use 2-5 dens, changing frequently and sharing some with others in areas of high population density. Usually solitary, they defend den sites marked by scent glands on the chin, chest and in the anal region, and have a home range up to 5.5 ha. Male home ranges may overlap those of several females. They are agile climbers and often travel long distances on the ground. Their vocal repertoire is extensive and includes loud chattering and screeching.
Development. Breeding occurs year round in the north, with peaks in autumn and spring in other areas. A single young is born 17-18 days after mating and attaches to one of two teats in the mother's forward-opening pouch, to which it remains attached for about 94 days, leaving the pouch at 140-150 days. Thereafter it is left in the den or rides on the mother's back until weaned at 6-7 months. Females are sexually mature at 12 months, males at 24 months, and live to 8 years or more. Many young males die trying to establish a home range.
Food. Eucalypt leaves, fruits, blossoms, grass, insects.
Habitat. All wooded areas including rainforests, and urban areas.
Status. Common.

Gymnobelideus leadbeateri

LEADBEATER'S POSSUM

Once presumed extinct, this arboreal marsupial was rediscovered in 1961. The soft fur is grey to greyish-brown above with a prominent dark brown stripe along the back, and paler below. The thick tail is broader and more bushy at the tip. The ears are thin, large and rounded with a small white patch at the base. They have striated footpads and retractable claws.
Size. Head-body: 150-170 mm. Tail: 145-180 mm.
Weight: 100-166 g.
Behaviour. Shy and secretive, they are nocturnal, resting in a communal nest of shredded bark more than 250 mm across placed in a large tree hollow with a narrow entrance. Colonies comprise up to eight animals with one monogamous breeding pair and their offspring. Females are evicted by the mother at 10 months old and forced to disperse and establish a new colony or join one which has lost its resident breeding female. Males may be allowed to stay or may be accepted by other colonies. They groom each other frequently and seem to recognise each other by smell, aggressively defending a territory of 1-2 ha against intruders. They climb smooth tree trunks easily and move quickly through the canopy, making leaps of 1-2 m between trees.
Development. They breed in all months except January and February, giving birth to 1-2 young, each attaching to one of four teats in the mother's rear-opening pouch. Females are independent at 10 months, males at 15 months.
Food. Insects and their exudates and plant exudates.
Habitat. Medium to high altitude sclerophyll forests with a dense understorey and large old or dead trees.
Status. Rare, scattered populations. Endangered by logging practices.

Trichosurus vulpecula

Gymnobelideus leadbeateri

Petauroides volans

The largest of the gliding possums, this species is a uniform greyish brown above with dark grey limbs in the north. Southern animals are variable, blackish-brown to sooty grey with a darker stripe along the centre of the back and flanks, or cream to greyish-white, sometimes with a pale head and tail. Both subspecies are white below. They have large ears with a furry fringe, a short snout and a square gliding membrane between the elbows and ankles. The tail is long, bushy and pendulous. The first two digits of the forefeet oppose the other three. The hindfeet have an opposing first toe; the second and third are fused with a double claw.

Size. Head-body: 350-450 mm. Tail: 450-600 mm. **Weight:** 0.9-1.8 kg

Behaviour. Active at night, they emerge from dens in tree hollows at dusk and follow established routes to feeding sites. Usually solitary, pairs often share dens during the mating season until the young leave the pouch. They have home ranges of 1-6 ha defined by scent-marking trees with anal gland secretions and urine. In good habitats males may have exclusive access to several females by defending an area that includes their home ranges. They are agile climbers and can glide more than 100 m, extending the limbs and bringing the paws under the chin. On the ground they have a clumsy loping gait. Females and their nestlings utter a high-pitched twittering sound when the mother approaches the den after foraging.

Development. Mating from February to May, females usually give birth to a single young that attaches to one of two teats in the forward-opening pouch for some 75 days. The infant leaves the pouch at about 5 months and rides on the mother's back or is left in the den until about 9 months old. Males are sexually mature at 12 months, females at 18 months.

Food. Eucalypt leaves and buds. They can exist without drinking.

Habitat. Wet and dry sclerophyll forests and tall woodlands.

Status. Common. Threatened by logging. Two subspecies: *P. v. volans* south of the Tropic of Capricorn; *P. v. minor* northern Australia.

Petaurus norfolcensis

Larger, but otherwise similar to the Sugar Glider, this species is light grey above with a dark stripe from the forehead along the back, and white to creamy-white below with white markings on the cheeks and behind the ears. The tail is broad, long, bushy and soft with a dark tip. They have large protruding eyes, large ears, a pointed muzzle and a rectangular gliding membrane between th hands and feet. The first two fingers of the forefeet oppose the other three. The hindfeet have an opposing first toe; the second and third are fused with a double claw.

Size. Head-body: 170-240 mm. Tail: 220-300 mm. **Weight:** 170-300 g.

Behaviour. Active mainly at night, they rest in leaf-lined nests in tree hollows in family groups with home ranges of 20-30 ha. They utter guttural chattering calls. They are agile climbers and can glide more than 50 m. **Development.** Sexually mature at about 12 months, they mate from May to December, usually giving birth to twins that attach to two of the four teats in the mother's forward-opening pouch. They vacate the pouch at about 70 days and are left in the nest for another 30 days before accompanying the mother on foraging trips until weaned at about 120 days.

Food. Acacia gum and eucalypt sap (released by scoring the bark with their sharp incisor teeth), insects and their exudates.

Habitat. Wet and dry sclerophyll forests and woodlands.

Status. Sparse. Two subspecies: *P. n. gracilis* north of Cardwell and *P. n. norfolcensis* in the south.

Petauroides volans

Petaurus norfolcensis

Petaurus breviceps

SUGAR GLIDER

Relatively small, this gliding possum is light grey above with a distinct dark stripe along the forehead and back, and dark patches behind the large pointed ears. It is creamy-white to pale grey below with short body fur and a bushy tail, sometimes white-tipped. A square gliding membrane joins the fifth finger and the first toe. The first two digits of the forefeet oppose the other three. The hindfeet have an opposing first toe, and the second and third are fused with a double claw.

Size. Head-body: 150-210 mm. Tail: 165-210 mm. **Weight:** 95-170 g.
Behaviour. Active mainly at night, they sleep in leaf-lined nests in tree hollows usually shared by a group of 2-7 adults and their young, comprising several females and a dominant male who scent-marks other group members and their territorial boundaries. Territories of about 1-5 ha are defended against intruders, and most juveniles of 7-10 months old are forced to disperse. In cold conditions they huddle together in the nest and become torpid for short periods when food is scarce. They are agile climbers and can glide more than 50 m, emitting a loud 'yip' alarm call and guttural calls when fighting. They defend food sources vigorously.
Development. Breeding from June to November, they may rear two sets of twins per season. Young are born 16 days after mating and attach to two of four teats in the forward-opening pouch for 40 days, emerging at 60-70 days. They remain in the nest until 100-110 days, and are weaned at 120 days. Females are sexually mature at 8-15 months, males at 12 months.
Food. Nectar, pollen, insects and their exudates, and tree exudates.
Habitat. Forests and woodlands.
Status. Common, with three subspecies in Australia and four in New Guinea.

Petaurus australis

YELLOW-BELLIED GLIDER

This rabbit-size gliding possum is dark to pale grey-brown above, off-white to yellow-orange below, with dark stripes along the mid back and thigh, and dark limbs. The ears are large, pointed and almost naked. The tail is long, broad and bushy. A square gliding membrane joins the wrists and ankles. The first two digits of the forefeet oppose the other three. The hindfeet have an opposing first toe, and the second and third are fused with a double claw.

Size. Head-body: 270-320 mm. Tail: 420-480 mm.
Weight: 450-700 g. Males are heavier and the northern race smaller.
Behaviour. Active mainly at night, they rest in nests in tree hollows lined with leaves carried in the coiled tail. They have exclusive home ranges of some 40-60 ha occupied by a monogamous pair and their offspring, often sharing a number of dens. Dominant northern males may live with up to five females and their young. They may travel more than 2 km for food, and occasionally feed in small groups in the same tree. Adults scent-mark family members. They emit loud shrieks, growls, whoos and rattling chatter. Very agile, they can run beneath branches and glide up to 120 m.
Development. Mating often takes place while clinging to the underside of a branch. Usually a single young is born between November and May (throughout the year in the northern subspecies). It attaches to one of two teats in the forward-opening pouch, where it stays for about 100 days, remaining in the nest for another 60 days and becoming independent at 180-240 days. Juveniles associate with the parents until sexually mature at 18-24 months.
Food. Nectar, pollen, insects, honeydew and sap obtained by biting into bark.
Habitat. Wet and dry sclerophyll forests and woodlands.
Status. Two subspecies: *P. a. australis* in the south is locally common; *P. a. reginae* in northern Queensland is rare and threatened by logging.

Petaurus breviceps

Petaurus australis

Acrobates pygmaeus

FEATHERTAIL GLIDER

A tiny, mouse-size arboreal marsupial, the Feathertail Glider derives its name from the flattened prehensile tail which has long stiff hairs on each side and closely resembles a feather. The fur is grey-brown above and white to cream below. A relatively small and thick gliding membrane extends from the elbows to the knees. The hindfeet have an opposing first toe and large gripping pads enabling them to cling to smooth vertical surfaces. The second and third toes fused with a double claw.
Size. Head-body: 65-80 mm. Tail: 60-80 mm. **Weight:** 10-17 g.
Behaviour. Active mainly at night, they sleep in spherical nests of leaves, ferns and bark strips in tree hollows or crevices. They form family groups of a male and one or two females and their offspring during the breeding season. Males are usually solitary at other times of the year. They use one or two nests and often share them with several others, huddling together in cold weather, and becoming torpid for several days when food is scarce. Feeding groups of up to 40 have been observed in profusely flowering trees. They are fast, agile and highly manoeuvrable in flight, leaping through the tree canopy and gliding more than 20 m, steering with the tail.
Development. They breed from July to January in the south and all year in the north, usually rearing several litters of 2-3 young in quick succession. Females have four teats in a forward-opening pouch where the young remain for 60-65 days, staying in the nest until weaned at 95-100 days. Females are sexually mature at 8-10 months, males at 12 months, and live for 3 years or more.
Food. Pollen, nectar, insects and sap.
Habitat. Wet and dry sclerophyll forests to woodlands.
Status. Common.

Dactylopsila trivirgata

STRIPED POSSUM

This striking, shy, slightly-built arboreal marsupial has contrasting black and white stripes from the nose to the base of the bushy tail, making a white Y-shaped pattern on the forehead. The belly is white, the limbs black-striped, and the tip of the pendulous tail is often white. They have large rounded ears, a large blunt head with long sharp lower incisor teeth and a long tongue. The hindfeet have an opposing first toe, the second and third are fused with a double claw. The fourth finger on each hand is about twice the length of the other four.
Size. Head-body: 240-270 mm. Tail: 310-340 mm. **Weight:** 240-400 g.
Behaviour. Active mainly at night, they sleep in leaf-lined nests in tree hollows or clumps of epiphytes. They are extremely agile and fast, leaping through the tree canopy in pursuit of rivals, and running with a peculiar lizard-like gait by swinging diagonally opposing limbs together. They are very noisy, emitting guttural shrieks when mating, snorting, rustling through the foliage, tearing at the bark, and making loud chewing and slurping sounds when feeding. When handled they emit a strong musky odour.
Development. Little is known about their development. Mating probably occurs between February and August. They give birth to one or two young. Females have two teats in a well-developed forward-opening pouch.
Food. Mostly wood-boring insects and larvae, extracted by biting into the bark and pulling them out with the long tongue or fourth finger. They also eat leaves, fruits, small vertebrates and the honey of native bees.
Habitat. Tropical rainforests and adjoining forests and woodlands.
Status. Sparse in a limited habitat threatened by logging; common in New Guinea.

Acrobates pygmaeus

Dactylopsila trivirgata

Cercartetus lepidus

The smallest of the possums, this tiny, mouse-sized arboreal marsupial is light grey-brown above and grey below with soft dense fur. The head is cone-shaped with broad oval ears and large eyes. The strongly prehensile tail tapers from a seasonally fat base to a sparsely-furred, pointed tip. Little Pygmy-possums can be distinguished from mice by their grasping hindfeet which have an opposing first toe and fused second and third toes forming a single digit with two claws.

Size. Head-body: 50-65 mm. Tail: 60-75 mm. **Weight:** 6-9 g.

Behaviour. Active at night, they sleep in abandoned bird nests or in roughly constructed nests of grass, leaves or shredded bark in tree hollows or crevices, stumps, among stones or forest debris. Solitary and cryptic, they stay in the lower levels of the forest or in thick scrub. They are fast agile climbers using the tail as a fifth limb. In cold conditions when food is short they curl up in a tight ball and become torpid for up to 6 days, lowering their body temperature to conserve energy and surviving on fat stored in the tail.

Development. Females become sexually mature in their first year and breed from August to January. Usually 2-3 young are born and attach to some of the four teats in the mother's shallow, forward-opening pouch. They vacate the pouch at about 6 weeks and are left in the nest or cling to the mother's back if she moves them until they are weaned at 12 weeks.

Food. Insects and their larvae, some pollen and small vertebrates. Prey is caught and manipulated with the forepaws.

Habitat. Mallee scrub, wet and dry sclerophyll forests and woodlands.

Status. Sparsely distributed. Threatened by logging.

Cercartetus nanus

The size of a large mouse, this arboreal marsupial has soft dense fur, fawn-grey to olive brown above and light grey to white below. The rounded head has very large eyes and ears and long whiskers. The prehensile tail has a seasonally fattened base, is almost naked and tapers to a fine point. The first toes of the hindfeet oppose the other three, the second and third are fused with a double claw.

Size. Head-body: 70-110 mm. Tail: 75-110 mm. **Weight:** 15-45 g.

Behaviour. Solitary and docile, they are predominantly nocturnal, sometimes emerging on overcast days. Small spherical nests about 60 mm across are constructed from shredded bark and located in hollows in tree trunks and stumps, under the bark of eucalypts or in the forks of tea trees. Several nests are used by individuals, and females may share them with their juvenile offspring. They are largely arboreal, moving at a moderate pace among foliage, sometimes suspending themselves by the tail. In cold conditions they become torpid for up to 12 days, conserving energy and using fat reserves stored in the tail. When provoked they utter a loud hiss.

Development. Sexually mature at 5 months, they give birth to four or five young between September and April, and may produce two litters per season. The pouch is shallow with four or five teats. The young are born some 30 days after mating and attach to the teats, quickly outgrowing the pouch and suckling while clinging to the mother's belly fur. They are left in the nest at about 42 days, are weaned at about 60 days, and may live more than 5 years.

Food. Pollen and nectar gathered with the brush-tipped tongue, insects and soft fruits.

Habitat. Open forests, heath and shrubland, rainforests.

Status. Common.

Cercartetus lepidus

Cercartetus nanus

Cercartetus concinnus WESTERN PYGMY-POSSUM

The size of a large mouse, this arboreal marsupial is smaller
than the Eastern Pygmy-possum and is fawn to reddish-brown
above with white belly fur. The head is conical with
large mobile ears, large eyes and very long whiskers.
The strongly prehensile tail has a seasonally-fattened
base, is naked for most of its length with fine scales,
and tapers to a point. It is coiled when not in use.
They can be distinguished from mice by their hindfeet
which have an opposing first toe and fused second and
third toes with a double claw.
Size. Head-body: 70-110 mm. Tail: 70-96 mm. **Weight:** 8-21 g.
Behaviour. Active mainly at night, they sleep in disused bird nests, among the
ground litter, or in a nest of shredded bark or leaves built in a tree hollow, stump,
or in the crown of a grass tree. Solitary and cryptic, they move quickly through the
foliage, occasionally leaping between branches and using their tail as a fifth limb.
On the ground they move quadrupedally. In cold conditions when food is short
they curl up in a tight ball and become torpid for periods up to 11 days, lowering
their body temperature and surviving on fat stored in the tail.
Development. Females are sexually mature at 12-15 months and breed throughout
the year, mating soon after giving birth, producing 2-3 litters per year. Usually four
young are born 50 days later and attach to four of the six teats in the mother's
forward-opening pouch, where they remain for some 30 days, thereafter being left
in the nest until weaned at 50 days.
Food. Insects, nectar and fruits, holding food in the forepaws.
Habitat. Dry sclerophyll forests and woodlands with a dense understorey, and
mallee heathlands.
Status. Common. Threatened by urban development.

Burramys parvus MOUNTAIN PYGMY-POSSUM

The only Australian mammal restricted to alpine and subalpine
areas, the Mountain Pygmy-possum is a largely terrestrial
rat-sized marsupial. The fine dense fur is grey-brown
above, sometimes darker along the mid back, pale grey
brown to cream below, and darker around the eyes. The
long, thin, scaly tail is covered with sparse fine hair
and appears naked. The hindfeet have an opposing first
toe, the second and third are fused with a double claw.
Size. Head-body: 100-120 mm. Tail: 130-160 mm. **Weight:** 30-60 g.
Behaviour. Active mainly at night, they sleep in nests of shredded
bark, leaves or grass carried in the curled tail and placed in crevices
or dense vegetation. Males and females share nests during the breeding season.
Males and juveniles are then forced out by the females, and are confined to poorer
habitats on the periphery of the breeding areas, causing a far higher mortality rate
among males. They climb among rocks and shrubs and move about along runways
under the snow in winter, hibernating for periods of 3-7 days.
Development. Females are sexually mature at 2 years and males at 1 year. They
breed from September to late December, producing more than four young 14-16
days after mating. Females have four teats in a forward-opening pouch, and only
the four newborn to attach to the teats survive. They vacate the pouch at 33-37
days, stay in the nest until 49-56 days old and become independent at 70-75 days.
The longest living of the small terrestrial mammals, they survive for more than 11
years in captivity.
Food. Insects, fruits and seeds manipulated with the hands while squatting. They
store seeds in the nest, under bark or beneath loose soil.
Habitat. Alpine heath, shrublands and woodlands above 1,400 m.
Status. Rare to locally common. Habitats are threatened by tourist development.

Cercartetus concinnus

Burramys parvus

Tarsipes rostratus

HONEY POSSUM

This mouse-size arboreal marsupial has a very long snout with a long, brush-tipped tongue used to probe into flowers. The fur is light brown to grey with three dark longitudinal stripes along the back, and cream below. The eyes are near the top of the head, the ears are rounded and the tail is long, thin, strongly prehensile and sparsely furred. The teeth are rudimentary pegs with two long, pointed lower incisors. The hands and feet have opposing first digits and large rough pads, the second and third toes of the hindfeet are fused and the claws are reduced to small nails.
Size. Head-body: 40-95 mm. Tail: 45-110 mm. **Weight**: 7-22 g. Females are usually larger than males.
Behaviour. Active mainly at night, they sleep in tree hollows, crevices or abandoned bird nests. They sometimes share nests and huddle together for warmth on cold days, becoming torpid for short periods when food is short. The largest female is dominant over other group members, including males to which she is most aggressive. They have overlapping home ranges of about 1 ha. Fast moving and agile, they dart rapidly between blossoms. They can walk below branches and climb vertically. They run quadrupedally with the tail straight out behind.
Development. Sexually mature at 6 months, with a life expectancy of 1-2 years, they breed most of the year, producing 2-3 litters of up to four young, born 21-28 days after mating. Newborn weigh about 5 mg and are the smallest mammalian young. They attach to the four teats in the forward-opening pouch, emerging at about 65 days, when they ride on the mother's back. They disperse after weaning at 90 days. Females may carry quiescent embryos.
Food. Pollen and nectar.
Habitat. Sandplain heaths and shrublands with suitable flowering plants.
Status. Common in appropriate habitats.

Cercartetus caudatus

LONG-TAILED PYGMY-POSSUM

The size of a large mouse, this arboreal marsupial is brownish grey above with a distinct dark eye patch, and pale grey below. The prehensile tail is long and thin with a furry, slightly thickened base. The head has a narrow pointed muzzle with a pink nose, large eyes and large thin ears. The first toe of the hindfoot is short and clawless with a bulbous tip and opposes the others. The second and third toes are fused with a double claw.
Size. Head-body: 100-110 mm. Tail: 125-150 mm. **Weight**: 20-40 g.
Behaviour. Active at night, they sleep in spherical nests of leaves or fern fronds in hollows in trees, stumps or fern clumps.
They are gregarious and cryptic in their habits. Females may share nests with their offspring or an adult male when not breeding (three females and one male were found in one nest). They forage alone or with 2-3 others. On cool winter days when food is scarce they become torpid to conserve energy. Agile climbers, they use the long prehensile tail as a fifth limb. When threatened they utter a throaty roar or a quiet defensive hiss.
Development. Sexually mature at 15 months, they mate all year with peaks in January and February and late August to early November, usually producing 2-3 young. Newborn each attach to one of the four teats in the mother's forward-opening pouch, which they vacate at about 34 days. They are weaned at about 80 days and become independent at 90 days.
Food. Nectar and insects.
Habitat. Tropical rainforests and open forests fringing rainforests.
Status. Common in a limited habitat. Threatened by logging. Extends to New Guinea.

Tarsipes rostratus

Cercartetus caudatus

Potorous tridactylus

LONG-NOSED POTOROO

This squat, rabbit-size, kangaroo-like marsupial has a prehensile
tail used to gather nesting material, well-developed upper
canine teeth and upper and lower incisor teeth that bite
against each other. The fur is grey to brown above (dark
rufous-brown in Tasmania) and paler below. They have a
long tapering nose with a naked tip, rounded ears and a
scaly tail furry at the base. The forelimbs are short
and muscular with forward-pointing toes with spatulate
claws. The second and third toes of the hindfeet are short
and fused with a double claw; the fourth is long and the fifth short.
Size. Head-body: 340-400 mm. Tail: 195-265 mm. **Weight:** 0.66-2.07 kg. Males are
larger than females.
Behaviour. Nocturnal, they sleep in simple nests of grass and other vegetation
carried in the curled tail and placed in scrapes below dense scrub, grass tussocks or
grass trees. During bush fires they seek refuge in the burrows of other animals.
Solitary and sedentary, they have overlapping home ranges of 5-10 ha, rarely
venture far from cover and sometimes gather in small groups. They move quickly
with a bipedal hopping gait assisted occasionally by the forelimbs, especially when
changing direction.
Development. Sexually mature at 12 months, they live to 12 years and breed all
year with peaks in summer and late winter. A single young is born 38 days after
mating and attaches firmly to one of four teats in the mother's pouch, leaving the
pouch by 15 weeks and suckling at foot for 5-6 weeks.
Food. Fungi, insects, roots, seeds, fruits. Digs in the soil with forelegs.
Habitat. Rainforest, open forest, woodlands with dense understorey to 1,600 m.
Status. Common, patchy distribution. Subspecies: *P. t. tridactylus* mainland
Australia; *P. t. apicalis* Tasmania and Bass Strait islands.

Hypsiprymnodon moschatus

MUSKY RAT-KANGAROO

This rat-size marsupial is the smallest macropod and the only
one with a mobile first toe on the hindfoot. The fur is
dense and soft, rich rufous-brown flecked with darker
hairs above, paler below with patches of white to cream
on the throat and chest. The tail is relatively short,
dark brown with small non-overlapping scales. The head
is long and slender with large rounded ears and a naked
nose. The hindfeet are relatively short with five toes,
sharp curved claws and striated pads on the palms and
soles; the second and third toes are fused at the base.
Size. Head-body: 153-307 mm. Tail: 123-165 mm. **Weight:** 337-680 g.
Behaviour. Active during the day, they forage in the early morning and late
afternoon, sleeping at midday and night in nests of dried grass, ferns and lichen
carried in the curled tail and built in clumps of lawyer vines, beneath tree
buttresses or in rock piles. They are solitary, sometimes feeding with one or two
others. They climb among fallen branches and move with a slow hop on the ground
with the tail held out behind, or run with a galloping gait, the hindfeet moving
forward outside the forelimbs..
Development. Sexually mature at about 12 months, they mate from February to
July. Courtship precedes mating by several days and includes standing erect, face-
to-face, touching their partner's head and neck with the forepaws. Females have
four teats and usually give birth to twins. Newborn attach firmly to teats in the
pouch, which they vacate about 21 weeks later and spend several more weeks in
the nest before accompanying the mother to feed.
Food. Insects, fruits and large seeds, manipulated with the forepaws.
Habitat. Tropical rainforests near creeks to 1,500 m.
Status. Reasonably common in a limited habitat. Threatened by logging.

Potorous tridactylus

Hypsiprymnodon moschatus

Bettongia penicillata

A squat, rabbit-size, kangaroo-like marsupial, the Brush-tailed Bettong has a prehensile tail used to gather nesting material, well-developed upper canine teeth and upper and lower incisor teeth that bite against each other. They are sandy-brown to yellow-grey above flecked with white and pale grey-brown to white below, with a black bushy tail tip. The broad head has a flattened naked nose and pointed ears. The short muscular forelimbs have forward-pointing toes with spatulate claws. The hindfeet have no first digit, the second and third are fused with a double claw, the fourth is much longer than the others.
Size. Head-body: 300-380 mm. Tail: 290-360 mm. **Weight**: 1.1-1.6 kg.
Behaviour. Nocturnal, they sleep in well-concealed domed nests of shredded bark and grass carried in the curled tail and constructed over shallow depressions dug under shrubs or other cover. They are solitary with large overlapping home ranges of 20 ha or more, and use 3-4 nests at random. They hop fast with the head held low, the back arched and the tail held out straight behind.
Development. Sexually mature at 5-6 months, they may live 4-6 years, breeding all year and producing 2-3 litters per year. Mating occurs soon after birth, although the embryo remains dormant until the pouch is empty. After a pregnancy of 21 days the newborn attaches to one of four teats in the mother's pouch, which it vacates at about 14 weeks and suckles at foot for 4 weeks.
Food. Underground fungi, bulbs, tubers, insects, seeds and resin. They can survive without drinking.
Habitat. Dry sclerophyll forests and woodlands with good cover to 300 m.
Status. Rare, scattered, endangered by land clearing and foxes.

Aepyprymnus rufescens

The largest bettong, this species has a prehensile tail, well developed upper canine teeth, and upper and lower incisor teeth that bite against each other. The head is broad with pointed ears and hairy muzzle. The fur is reddish brown to grey-brown flecked with light grey above and white below. The short muscular forelimbs have forward pointing toes with long curved claws. The hindfeet have no first digit, the second and third are fused with a double claw, the fourth is much longer than the others.
Size. Head-body: 375-390 mm. Tail: 335-390 mm. **Weight**: to 3.5 kg.
Behaviour. Nocturnal, they sleep in spherical to cone-shaped nests with a single entrance made of grass collected in the mouth and carried in the curled tail, constructed over shallow depressions at the base of tussocks or under logs. Individuals have clusters of nests often close to a feeding site, used randomly and abandoned if disturbed. They have overlapping home ranges of some 20 ha, and may feed in small groups, hopping quickly with the forelegs tucked in against the body, and standing with the head withdrawn and the back arched. When alarmed they stand upright with the arms held stiffly by their sides and stamp their hindfeet as they hop away. Vocalisations include low hisses when alarmed and growls and grunts when interacting socially.
Development. Sexually mature at 9-12 months, they breed throughout the year and mate soon after birth, although the embryo remains dormant until the pouch is vacated. After a pregnancy of 22-24 days a single young is born and attaches to one of four teats in the mother's pouch. The pouch is vacated at 14-16 weeks and the young suckles at foot for 7 weeks.
Food. Grass, roots, herbs and tubers dug up with the forefeet.
Habitat. Grassy open forests to 700 m.
Status. Common. Threatened by land clearing.

Bettongia penicillata

Aepyprymnus rufescens

Bettongia gaimardi

TASMANIAN BETTONG

Extinct on the mainland, the Tasmanian Bettong is still widespread
in Tasmania. It has a prehensile tail used to carry nesting
material, well-developed upper canine teeth, and upper
and lower incisor teeth that bite against each other.
The broad head has rounded ears and a naked nose. The
fur is coarse with soft underfur, brownish-grey flecked
with dark brown to black above, and greyish-white below.
The tail is well-furred, dark brown towards the end with
a white tip. The short muscular forelimbs have forward
pointing toes with long curved claws. The hindfeet have no first
digit, the second and third are fused with a double claw, the fourth
is much longer than the others.
Size. Head-body: 315-350 mm. Tail: 285-350 mm. **Weight:** 1.2-2.3 kg.
Behaviour. Nocturnal, they sleep in ovoid nests about 300 mm long of densely
woven dry grass and bark collected in the mouth, carried in the curled tail and
manipulated with the snout. Nests have a single entrance and are constructed over
shallow depressions concealed under shrubs, tussocks or logs, and may be used for
more than one month. They have anal scent-producing glands probably used to
mark the nest site. Usually solitary, they have home ranges of up to 135 ha, and
travel more than 1 km to feeding sites.
Development. Sexually mature at 8-11 months, they breed throughout the year
and mate soon after the birth, although the embryo remains dormant until the
pouch is vacated. After a pregnancy of 21-22 days a single young is born and
attaches to one of four teats in the mother's pouch. The pouch is vacated at 14-16
weeks and the young suckles at foot for 8-9 weeks.
Food. Fungi, seeds, roots and bulbs dug up with the forefeet.
Habitat. Dry sclerophyll forests with a grassy understorey to 1,000 m.
Status. Common.

Lagorchestes conspicillatus

SPECTACLED HARE-WALLABY

A stout, short-necked marsupial, the Spectacled Hare-wallaby
derives its name from the rufous-brown rings surrounding
the eyes. They are brown flecked with white above and
white below, with white stripes on the hips. The tail
is sparsely-haired and darker towards the tip. The face
is square viewed from the front with a black nose and
pointed ears. The long hindfeet have no first digit,
the second and third are fused with a double claw, and
the fourth is much longer than the others.
Size. Head-body: 400-470 mm. Tail: 370-490 mm. **Weight:** 1.6-4.5 kg.
Behaviour. Nocturnal, they sleep in cool hides tunnelled into grass
tussocks, spinifex hummocks, or formed in clumps of porcupine grass.
Predominantly solitary, they may feed with one or two others, and occupy home
ranges of 9-10 ha with several hides. They can move fast and have a powerful
jumping ability. Vocalisations include a soft clicking and a warning hiss. They
conserve water in hot dry conditions by raising their body temperature and eating
less food, reducing the amount of water needed for evaporative cooling and
digestion.
Development. Sexually mature at 12 months, they breed all year, although
development of the embryo is delayed in drought conditions and when the mother
has a pouch young. A single young is born and attaches firmly to one of the four
teats in the mother's pouch. The pouch is vacated at about 5 months.
Food. Leaves, native grasses. Can survive without water.
Habitat. Tropical grasslands, open forests, woodlands, arid grasslands and
shrublands.
Status. Common in Queensland and Barrow Island, scattered elsewhere. Desert
populations collapse in drought conditions and recover in good years.

Bettongia gaimardi

Lagorchestes conspicillatus

Petrogale lateralis

BLACK-FOOTED ROCK-WALLABY

Found in arid and semi-arid areas of central and western Australia, the Black-footed Rock-wallaby has thick soft fur, reddish-brown to purple above, pale yellow-brown below, grey to purple on the neck and shoulders, with a black stripe from the back of the head to the mid-back and sometimes with white cheek and side stripes. The feet are dark brown and the tail has a dark brown to black tip. The hindfeet have no first digit, the second and third are fused with a double claw, and the claw of the long fourth toe projects only slightly beyond the large pad. The pads are granulated with a fringe of stiff hairs.
Size. Head-body: 450-550 mm. Tail: 450-610 mm. **Weight:** 4-6 kg.
Behaviour. Nocturnal, they shelter in caves and rocky crevices, emerging in the late afternoon or evening to feed. In cool weather they may bask in the sun. They are gregarious and form colonies with separate male and female dominance hierarchies established mainly by ritualised and aggressive acts, including kicking, but rarely actually fighting. They hop with great agility on rocky outcrops with the tail arched over the back.
Development. Females are sexually mature at 12-24 months and mate soon after giving birth to a single young, although development of the embryo is delayed until the pouch is vacated. The newborn attaches firmly to one of four teats in the mother's pouch.
Food. Grasses and other vegetable matter.
Habitat. Semi-arid to arid rocky granite outcrops with mallee and other scrub and tussock grassland, often in montane areas.
Status. Locally common to rare.

Petrogale penicillata

BRUSH-TAILED ROCK-WALLABY

Previously confused with *P. inornata* (found north of Rockhampton) this species has a dull brown back, a rufous rump, black furry feet and a long densely-furred tail with a bushy tip. Southern animals have a black tail and armpits, pale stripes along the sides, white cheek stripes, a black stripe on the forehead, and black patches on the ears which are yellowish inside with whitish margins. The hindfeet have no first digit, the second and third are fused with a double claw, and the claw of the long fourth toe projects only slightly beyond the large pad. The pads are granulated with a fringe of stiff hairs.
Size. Head-body: 450-580 mm. Tail: 520-670 mm. **Weight:** 4-7.6 kg. Males are larger than females.
Behaviour. Nocturnal, they shelter in caves, rocky crevices and dense stands of Lantana, forming colonies with dominance hierarchies. Individuals have overlapping home ranges with exclusive den sites. Females frequently share and defend den sites, usually with relatives, and groom each other regularly. Young at foot are left behind while the mother travels long distances for food or drink. They hop with great agility on rocky outcrops with the tail arched over the back, and are able to climb sloping tree trunks.
Development. Females are sexual mature by 18 months, males by 20 months. They breed all year, mating soon after giving birth, although development of the embryo is delayed until the pouch is vacated. After a pregnancy of 31 days a single young is born and attaches to one of four teats in the pouch, where it remains for about 29 weeks, thereafter suckling for some 3 months.
Food. Leaves, sedges, ferns, roots, bark, fruit and grasses.
Habitat. Rocky sites in sclerophyll forests with a grassy understorey.
Status. Common. Subspecies: *P. p. penicillata* NSW and Vic.; *P. p. herberti* Qld.

Petrogale lateralis

Petrogale penicillata

Petrogale brachyotis

SHORT-EARED ROCK-WALLABY

Although abundant and distributed over a wide area, little is known about the biology of the Short-eared Rock-wallaby. The fur is short and fine, light grey above and white to greyish-white below. They have a dark brown neck stripe, a white shoulder patch and dark tip to the tail. Arnhem Land individuals are dark grey to brown above with a distinct white or buff side stripe, a dark neck and back stripe. The ears are less than half the length of the head and have a whitish margin. The hindfeet have no first digit, the second and third are fused with a double claw, and the fourth is much longer than the others.

Size. Head-body: 410-520 mm. Tail: 420-550 mm. **Weight**: to 5.6 kg. Males are larger than females.

Behaviour. Nocturnal, they sleep in cool rocky crevices, emerging in the evening to feed in adjacent areas, often with others.

Development. Nothing is known about their development. They probably breed throughout the year with a peak in the wet season, giving birth to a single young which attaches to one of the four teats in the mother's pouch.

Food. Predominantly leaves and seeds with a small amount of grass.

Habitat. Low rocky hills, cliffs and gorges with open forest, scrub and grasslands.

Status. Common to scattered.

Petrogale xanthopus

YELLOW-FOOTED ROCK-WALLABY

A very attractively ornamented and brightly-coloured species, the Yellow-footed Rock-wallaby has a greyish-fawn back with rich brown stripes along the centre of the back, hips and arms, white stripes along the cheeks and sides, rufous-brown arms and legs, white underparts, and a rufous-brown tail with dark bands. The ears are long and the nose naked. The hindfeet have no first digit, the second and third are fused with a double claw, and the fourth is much longer than the others. The claw of the fourth toe projects only slightly beyond the large pad. The pads are granulated for gripping, with a fringe of stiff hairs around them.

Size. Head-body: 490-650 mm. Tail: 560-700 mm. **Weight**: 6-8 kg. Males are larger than females.

Behaviour. Active mainly at night, they bask in the sun in winter and shelter during the day under rocky outcrops or among vegetation between boulders, emerging in the evening to feed. They are gregarious, forming colonies and occupying defined home ranges. Males establish dominance hierarchies by ritualised aggressive acts and occasionally fighting. They are agile, hopping among rocks with the tail arched over the back, and are able to climb sloping tree trunks. The young are left behind in a safe place while the mother travels long distances for food or drink. The young make a clicking call when lost or disturbed.

Development. Females reach sexual maturity between 11 and 22 months, males at about 30 months. They may breed throughout the year and mate soon after birth, although development of the embryo is delayed until the pouch is vacated. After a pregnancy of 31-33 days a single young is born and attaches to one of the four teats in the mother's pouch, where it remains for about 28 weeks, thereafter suckling at foot until weaned.

Food. Mainly leaves with some grass and herbs. They need access to water, drinking frequently in hot weather.

Habitat. Arid rocky sites with open woodland and scrub.

Status. Common in limited areas. Subspecies: *P. x. celeris* Queensland; *P. x. xanthopus* elsewhere.

Petrogale brachyotis

Petrogale xanthopus

Thylogale stigmatica RED-LEGGED PADEMELON

A small compact macropod generally found in densely vegetated habitats, the Red-legged Pademelon has thick soft fur, grey-brown to dark brown above with red-brown markings on the cheeks, thighs and forearms. The ears are rounded, the nose naked and the tail short and thick. The hindfeet have no first digit, the second and third are fused with a double claw, and the fourth is much longer than the others.
Size. Head-body: 385-540 mm. Tail: 300-475 mm.
Weight: 2.5-6.8 kg. Males are larger than females.
Behaviour. Nocturnal, they sleep in refuges in dense cover, sitting with the tail between the legs, leaning back on a rock or tree and sleeping with the head on the tail or ground. They emerge in the late afternoon to forage until early morning, following runways through the ground vegetation to feeding sites. They are shy, normally solitary, sometimes feeding with 1-3 others. Females make a rasping sound when rejecting courtship advances by a male; males make a soft clucking during courtship, a sound similar to that used by females calling their young.
Development. Their reproduction has not been studied. Females have a well-developed pouch with four teats and give birth to a single young.
Food. Fallen leaves, fruit, ferns, fungi, native grasses.
Habitat. Rainforests, wet sclerophyll forests and vine scrubs.
Status. Common, widespread. Subspecies: *T. s. stigmatica* Cairns region; *T. s. coxenii* Cape York; *T. s. wilcoxi* southern Qld and NSW. Extends to New Guinea.

Thylogale thetis RED-NECKED PADEMELON

The Red-necked Pademelon is a compact macropod of the forest edge and can be distinguished from the Red-legged Pademelon by the reddish-brown fur around the neck and shoulders. The thick soft fur is brownish-grey on the back and whitish below. The ears are rounded, the nose naked and the tail short and thick. The hindfeet have no first digit, the second and third are fused with a double claw, and the fourth is much longer than the others.
Size. Head-body: 290-620 mm. Tail: 270-510 mm.
Weight: 1.8-9.2 kg. Males are larger than females.
Behaviour. Active at various times, they generally feed in forest clearings at night, travelling through the forest by day seeking food, and basking in the sun in winter. They rest in shallow depressions in the leaf litter in dense cover, moving along well-defined runways to feeding sites. Males establish dominance hierarchies by fighting or ritualised aggression. They have home ranges of 5-30 ha and often aggregate on pastures close to the forest edge at night where their home ranges overlap, dispersing during the day. Slow movements are quadrupedal with the tail dragging behind. When hopping they hold the tail out stiffly behind. Vocalisations include a threatening growl and clucking by females calling their young and by males during courtship. If alarmed they thump their hindfeet as they hop away.
Development. Sexually mature at 17 months, they breed all year with peaks in autumn and spring in northern areas and January-February in the south. A single young is born and attaches to one of the four teats in the mother's pouch, vacating the pouch by 26 weeks and suckling at foot for some 4 weeks.
Food. Grasses, herbs and leaves, often holding food in the forepaws.
Habitat. Margins of closed forests and rainforests.
Status. Common.

Thylogale stigmatica

Thylogale thetis

Setonix brachyurus

A small robust wallaby, the Quokka has long, thick and coarse
fur flecked grey and brown with a rufous tinge above and
pale grey below. A dark stripe may be seen on the forehead.
The head is broad with small rounded ears set on top.
The tail is thick and sparsely-haired with visible
scales. The hindfeet have no first digit, the second
and third are fused with a double claw, and the fourth
is much longer than the others.
Size. Head-body: 400-540 mm. Tail: 245-310 mm. **Weight:**
2.4-3.3 kg.
Behaviour. Active mainly at night, they rest in dense vegetation
within overlapping home ranges of around 4 ha. Males defend areas around their
nest sites and may form long term bonds with females. Adults converge at night
around waterholes within a group territory occupied an defended by 25-150 adults,
who may fight for available water in dry conditions. Adult males establish
dominance hierarchies according to age. Females and juveniles have no rank. They
move with a bounding gait interspersed with short high-speed hopping bouts, and
may climb into trees to reach twigs up to 2 m high.
Development. Females are sexually mature at 18-24 months and breed throughout
the year on the mainland. On Rottnest Island breeding takes place from January to
August. After a pregnancy of 25-28 days a single young is born and attaches to one
of four teats in the mother's pouch. Young vacate the pouch by 26 weeks and
suckle at foot for 2 months, living to 10 years or more.
Food. Grasses, leaves and succulents. They can survive for long periods without
water and have been reported to be able to drink seawater.
Habitat. Wet and dry sclerophyll forests, woodlands and heath.
Status. Common on Rottnest Island, rare on the mainland.

Thylogale billardierii

A small, stockily-built macropod, the Tasmanian Pademelon is now
extinct in southeastern South Australia and Victoria. The
dense fur is long and soft, dark brown to golden-brown
with a grey base above, and pale reddish-buff below with
a grey to white base. The tail is short and thick, the
ears rounded and the nose naked. The hindfeet have no
first digit, the second and third are fused with a double
claw, and the fourth is much longer than the others.
Size. Head-body: 360-720 mm. Tail: 320-485 mm. **Weight:** 2.4-12 kg.
Males are much larger and more muscular than females.
Behaviour. Nocturnal, they take refuge in dense cover and have home
ranges as large as 170 ha, travelling along well-established runways to feeding sites
up to 2 km away. Males establish dominance hierarchies by fighting and ritualised
aggression, giving top-ranking males exclusive mating rights with females during
the breeding season. They often feed in groups of 10 or more, rarely venturing more
than 100 m from the forest edge. They have a short rapid hop and escape to the
dense undergrowth when alarmed. Males utter a guttural growl or hiss when
fighting and make clucking sounds during courtship.
Development. Sexually mature at about 14 months, the majority of births occur
from April to June. Females mate soon after giving birth, although development of
the embryo is delayed until the pouch is vacated. After a pregnancy of 30 days a
single young is born and attaches to one of four teats in the mother's pouch. Young
leave the pouch at about 29 weeks and suckle at foot for a further 11 weeks.
Food. Grasses, herbs and leaves, often held food in the forepaws. In winter they dig
vegetation out of the snow.
Habitat. Coastal and montane forests, densely vegetated with grassy areas.
Status. Common.

Setonix brachyurus

Thylogale billardierii

Dendrolagus lumholtzi

Found in the rainforests of northeastern Australia, this unusual kangaroo is blackish-brown above with lighter flecks on the rump, black paws and a pale band across the forehead and down the sides of the face. The tail is long and thick but not prehensile. The ears are very small and rounded. The limbs are shorter than other kangaroos. The forelimbs are stout and muscular with strong curved claws and an opposing first digit. The toes on the hindfeet are a similar length with uniformly granular soles and strong curved claws, the second and third toes are fused at the base with a double claw used for grooming.

Size. Head-body: 480-590 mm. Tail: 600-740 mm. **Weight:** 3.7-10 kg. Males are larger than females.

Behaviour. Nocturnal, they sleep crouched on a branch in the crown of a tree and climb through the canopy with the tail hanging loosely, gripping with the clawed forefeet and balancing with the hindfeet. The hindlegs move independently when climbing or walking along a branch. They hop along broad branches and jump from tree to tree or descend backwards, jumping down from at least 2 m to land on the feet. On the ground they walk or run quadrupedally and hop with the forelegs tucked into the body and the tail held out stiffly. Usually solitary, they sometimes feed with up to three others. Males fight if they are kept together, and make a clucking sound during courtship.

Development. Little is known about their development. They probably breed all year and give birth to a single young.

Food. Leaves supplemented by fruits.

Habitat. Tropical rainforests.

Status. Common in limited area. Threatened by logging.

Dendrolagus bennettianus

Similar in many respects to Lumholtz's Tree-kangaroo, this arboreal marsupial of the rainforests of northeastern Australia is dark brown above and light fawn below with a rusty brown area on the back of the head and shoulders. The forehead and muzzle are greyish, the feet, hands and base of the tail are black, the long tail has a bushy tip and a light brown patch on the upper surface. The ears are small and rounded. The forelimbs are stout and muscular with strong curved claws and an opposing first digit. The toes on the relatively short hindfeet are a similar length with granular soles and strong curved claws, the second and third toes are fused at the base with a double claw for grooming.

Size. Head-body: 500-650 mm. Tail: 630-940 mm. **Weight:** to 13 kg. Males are much larger than females.

Behaviour. Nocturnal, they sleep crouched on a tree branch and climb through the canopy at night with the tail hanging loosely, gripping with the clawed forefeet and balancing with the hindfeet. The hindlegs move independently when climbing or walking along a branch. They hop along broad branches and jump from tree to tree or descend backwards, jumping down from at least 2 m to land on the feet. On the ground they walk or run quadrupedally or hop, often travelling long distances. Usually solitary, family groups of male, female and young at foot have been seen. They growl when alarmed and females call their young with soft trumpeting sounds.

Development. Details of their breeding and development are not known. They probably breed all year and give birth to a single young.

Food. Leaves supplemented by fruits.

Habitat. Tropical rainforests and occasionally open forests.

Status. Sparse in remaining habitat. Threatened by logging.

Dendrolagus lumholtzi

Dendrolagus bennettianus

Onychogalea unguifera NORTHERN NAILTAIL WALLABY

Characterised by a small horny spur of unknown function hidden among a brush of dark hairs at the end of their slender whip-like tail, this wallaby has sandy brown fur with a dark lower back stripe extending along the tail, and a faint dark shoulder stripe. The muzzle is squarish and the ears long. The upper incisor teeth are very slender and inclined forward. The forefeet have long, well-developed claws. The long hindfeet have no first digit, the second and third are fused with a double claw, and the fourth is much longer than the others.

Size. Head-body: 490-690 mm. Tail: 600-730 mm. **Weight:** 4.5-9 kg. Males are larger than females.

Behaviour. Active mainly at night, they rest in grassy tussocks or under low trees or shrubs, excavating a scrape in the soil with their forefeet. Generally solitary, they may feed with 1-3 others, travelling more than 3 km from daytime resting sites to feeding areas, staying close to shelter. They move with a low crouching hop with an upcurved tail, and move the forelimbs in an unusual rotary action during rapid movement.

Development. Little is known about their development. Females give birth to a single young which attaches firmly to one of four teats in the mother's pouch.

Food. Leaves, native grasses, herbs, fruits, stem bases and rhizomes.

Habitat. Open grassy woodlands, grasslands and shrubby savannah, usually near water.

Status. Common.

Macropus antilopinus ANTILOPINE WALLAROO

A large marsupial of the tropical northern woodlands, the Antilopine Wallaroo derives its name from the long, fine, supposedly antelope-like fur. They are reddish sandy-brown above, very pale brown to white below, often with pale patches on the legs and tail. Females may be bluish-grey. The paws are black, the nose is naked and the tail relatively short and thick. The hindfeet have no first digit, the second and third are fused with a double claw, and the fourth is much longer than the others.

Size. Head-body: 775-1200 mm. Tail: 675-890 mm. **Weight:** 16-49 kg. Males are much larger and more powerfully built than females.

Behaviour. Active at night and during cool days, they rest in the shade of trees, shrubs or rocks, usually near a waterhole. They are gregarious, usually in groups of 3-8, forming larger groups if threatened. Males are often seen alone probably searching for female mates. Group membership changes frequently and males groom each other regularly. When alarmed they hiss and thump the ground with their hindfeet as they hop rapidly away.

Development. They breed throughout the year, with a peak of mating activity in the early wet season. A single young is born some 34 days after mating and attaches firmly to one of the four teats in the mother's pouch, vacating the pouch permanently at about 38 weeks, thereafter suckling at foot until about 12 months old.

Food. Native grasses.

Habitat. Open savannah woodlands and open monsoonal forests, usually in flat or undulating country.

Status. Common.

Onychogalea unguifera

Macropus antilopinus.

Macropus agilis

Alert and nervous, the Agile Wallaby is often seen along the tropical coast of Australia. Sandy brown above and light buff to whitish below, they have a whitish stripe along the cheek and thigh, a dark brown stripe down the forehead, a long black tipped tail and black edged ears. The long pointed face has a partially naked muzzle. The hindfeet lack a first digit, the second and third are fused with a double claw, the fourth is much longer than the others.

Size. Head-body: 593-850 mm. Tail: 587-840 mm. **Weight:** 9-29 kg. Males are much larger and more muscular than females.

Behaviour. Active during the late afternoon and night, Agile Wallabies rest alone or in small groups in dense vegetation. Although essentially solitary animals, they come together in feeding groups when food is short and to mate. When threatened they thump their hind feet and hop rapidly away with the head held high, the tail horizontal and the forearms extended.

Development. Females are sexually mature at 12 months, males at about 14 months, and live to 12 years. They breed throughout the year. Females mate soon after giving birth, producing a single embryo that remains dormant until the pouch is empty. After a pregnancy of 29-31 days, the newborn attaches firmly to one of four teats in the mother's pouch, which it vacates by 31 weeks, thereafter suckling at foot until 10-12 months old.

Food. Grasses, sedges, leaves, fruits and roots dug up with the forepaws.

Habitat. Open forests, coastal sand dunes and along creeks.

Status. Common. Extends to New Guinea.

Macropus rufogriseus

The Red-necked Wallaby has soft deep fur, dark brown to reddish brown above with pale tan to white tips and reddish-brown on the neck. The belly and chest are light grey, the upper lip has a white stripe, the nose, paws and longest toe are black. Females are paler, although both sexes on Tasmania and the Bass Strait Islands are darker. The tail is well-furred with a brushy tip. The hindfeet have no first digit, the second and third are fused with a double claw, and the fourth is much longer than the others.

Size. Head-body: 660-925 mm. Tail: 620-880 mm. **Weight:** 11-27 kg. Males are larger than females.

Behaviour. They rest in dense vegetation, emerging in the late afternoon or earlier on cool days, and follow well-defined runways to feeding sites. Males have home ranges of about 32 ha. Female home ranges are around 12 ha and overlap those of close female relatives. Males establish dominance hierarchies by fighting and ritualised aggressive acts. They range widely searching for females in oestrous, although subordinate males are excluded from mating by dominant males and the females. Young males are forced out of their mother's territory at about 2 years of age, whereas female offspring may settle in adjoining home ranges.

Development. Females are sexually mature at 11-21 months, males at 13-19 months, and may live to 18 years. Mainland animals breed throughout the year, those in Tasmania breed from January to August. Females mate soon after giving birth, the embryo remaining dormant until the pouch is empty, or in Tasmania until the next breeding season. One or two young are born after a pregnancy of 29-30 days. Newborn attach firmly to one of four teats in the mother's pouch, which they vacate at 40 weeks and suckling at foot until 12 to 17 months old.

Food. Native grasses.

Habitat. Sclerophyll forests, woodlands with dense understoreys, heathlands.

Status. Common.

Macropus agilis

Macropus rufogriseus

Macropus parma

PARMA WALLABY

A cryptic inhabitant of forests with thick shrubby understoreys, the Parma Wallaby has thick fur, grey-brown to dark brown above with a dark stripe from the head to the mid-back, and white stripes along the upper lip, throat, chest and belly. Many have a white-tipped tail. The faecal pellets are flattened and square to rectangular. The hindfeet have no first digit, the second and third are fused with a double claw, the fourth is much longer than the others.
Size. Head-body: 445-530 mm. Tail: 405-545 mm. **Weight:** 3.2-5.9 kg. Males are larger with more robust arms and chest.
Behaviour. Active mainly at night, they rest under shrubs in dense vegetation, travelling along established runways to graze in small grassy areas. Generally solitary, they sometimes congregate in small feeding groups with 2-3 others. They hop close to the ground, almost horizontally, with the forearms tucked into the body sides and the tail curved up slightly. Vocalisations include clucking and hissing sounds.
Development. Females are sexually mature at 16 months, males at 22 months. The breeding season extends throughout the year with most births from February to June. They usually mate 45-105 days after giving birth, the embryo remaining dormant until the pouch is empty. After a pregnancy of 33-36 days the newborn attaches firmly to one of four teats in the mother's pouch, which it vacates at about 30 weeks, suckling at foot until about 10 months old.
Food. Grasses and herbs.
Habitat. Rainforests and sclerophyll forests with a dense understorey and grassy areas, normally in montane areas.
Status. Rare, scattered, probably underestimated.

Wallabia bicolor

SWAMP WALLABY

The Swamp Wallaby is distinguished from the other wallabies of eastern Australia by its very dark colour. The fur is coarse, dark brown to black flecked with yellow above and light red-brown to yellow-brown below. The cheeks and shoulders have a light yellow to red-brown or black stripe; the paws, feet and occasionally the end of the tail are very dark brown. The hindfeet have no first digit, the second and third are fused with a double claw, and the fourth is much longer than the others.
Size. Head-body: 665-850 mm. Tail: 640-865 mm. **Weight:** 10-22 kg. Males are larger than females.
Behaviour. They are active both day and night, resting in thick undergrowth, remaining in dense cover during the day and moving out to more open grassy areas at night. Generally solitary, they have home ranges of up to 6 ha or more and sometimes feed with one or two others. Moving slowly they often seem relatively uncoordinated with the tail held high, often making high leaps in long grass. Moving fast they hold the head low and the tail horizontal.
Development. Sexual maturity is reached at 15-18 months with a lifespan of about 15 years. They have no defined breeding season. Females mate about 7 days before giving birth, producing a single embryo that remains dormant until the pouch is empty. After a pregnancy of 33-38 days the newborn attaches firmly to one of the four teats in the mother's pouch, which it vacates at about 36 weeks, thereafter suckling at foot until some 15 months old.
Food. Shrubs, pine seedlings, rushes, fungi, vines, ferns and grasses.
Habitat. Rainforests, sclerophyll forests and woodlands with a dense understorey, and heathland.
Status. Common.

Macropus parma

Wallabia bicolor

Macropus eugenii

One of the smallest wallabies, the Tammar Wallaby has long soft fur, dark grey-brown flecked with light grey above, with reddish-brown patches on the flanks and limbs, and paler below with a white muzzle, a white stripe on the cheek and a dark stripe down the forehead. The ears are slightly pointed and the nose is naked. The hindfeet have no first digit, the second and third are fused with a double claw, and the fourth is much longer than the others.

Size. Head-body: 520-680 mm. Tail: 330-450 mm. **Weight:** 4-10 kg. Males are larger than females. Island populations differ in size and colouration.

Behaviour. They are usually active for a few hours after dusk and again in the hours before dawn, sleeping in low dense vegetation and moving along established runways or paths to grassy feeding sites up to 1 km away. They are solitary with defined overlapping home ranges of some 30 ha, and may be seen feeding with one or two others.

Development. Females are sexually mature at about 8 months while still suckling, males at 24 months. They live to 11 years or more, although juveniles have a high mortality rate in their first summer, particularly if dry conditions follow a wet cold winter. Females give birth to a single young from January to July. They mate soon after giving birth, and the embryo typically remains dormant until late December. After a pregnancy of 29 days the newborn attaches firmly to one of four teats in the mother's pouch, vacating the pouch permanently at about 36 weeks, and suckling at foot until about 9 months old.

Food. Native grasses. They are able to survive by drinking seawater in drought conditions.

Habitat. Dry sclerophyll forests and woodlands, mallee and coastal scrub, heathlands.

Status. Common in a limited habitat. Threatened by clearing of scrub and introduced predators.

Macropus irma

Although common over much of its range, the Western Brush Wallaby has not been studied in detail. They are pale grey above sometimes tinged with brown with black and white ear margins, a white stripe from the ear to nose a crest of black hair along the long tail, and faint barring on the back and tail some individuals . The hindfeet have no first digit, the second and third are fused with a double claw, and the fourth is much longer than the others.

Size. Head-body: 830-1530 mm. Tail: 540-970 mm. **Weight:** 7-9 kg.

Behaviour. More diurnal than many of the other macropods, they are active during the late afternoon and early morning, resting during the night and in the hotter part of the day alone or in pairs in the shade or in clumps of vegetation. They are fast with good manoeuvrability, hopping with the head held low and the tail straight out behind.

Development. Females usually giving birth to a single young in April or May. The newborn attaches firmly to one of the four teats in the mother's pouch, vacating the pouch permanently at about 7 months and then suckling at foot.

Food. Native grasses. They can survive without drinking.

Habitat. Dry sclerophyll forests, particularly Jarrah; woodlands, preferably with scrubby thickets and wet sites; heathland and mallee scrub.

Status. Common.

Macropus eugenii

Macropus irma

Macropus dorsalis

BLACK-STRIPED WALLABY

A shy macropod seldom venturing far from cover, this wallaby can
be distinguished by the black stripe extending from the neck
to rump, the sandy to reddish-brown back, paler flanks,
white thigh stripes and white cheek patch. The tail is
sparsely-haired and scaly. The hindfeet have no first
digit, the second and third are fused with a double
claw, and the fourth is much longer than the others.
Size. Head-body: 1120-1590 mm. Tail: 540-830 mm.
Weight: 6-20 kg. Males are much larger than females.
Behaviour. Active mainly at night, they rest in dense vegetation
in groups of 20 or more, travelling in single file from the resting
site along established runways to grazing areas. Adults groom and lick each other
frequently and probably establish dominance hierarchies through sparring
encounters. They flee if disturbed, moving with a short hopping gait with the back
curved, the head low and forearms extended out from the body.
Development. Females are sexually mature at 14 months, males at 20 months, with
a life span of 10-15 years. Breeding year round, females mate soon after giving
birth, although the embryo remains dormant until the pouch is empty. A single
young is born after a pregnancy of 33-35 days. The newborn attaches firmly to one
of the four teats in the mother's pouch, which it vacates at 30 weeks, thereafter
suckling at foot until weaned.
Food. Native grasses.
Habitat. Closed and open forests with a thick understorey.
Status. Common.

Macropus parryi

WHIPTAIL WALLABY

This slim graceful macropod has a triangular face with large brown
and white ears, a dark brown forehead and a contrasting
white cheek stripe. The winter coat is light grey above and
the summer coat brownish-grey. They are white below
with a light brown stripe along the neck and shoulder,
a white stripe on the hip, dark paws and a dark tip to
the long slender tail. The hindfeet have no first digit,
the second and third are fused with a double claw, and
the fourth is much longer than the others.
Size. Head-body: 675-955 mm. Tail: 725-1045 mm. **Weight:** 7-26 kg.
Males are larger and stronger than females.
Behaviour. Active mainly during the early morning and late afternoon, they rest in
shady sites. Dominance hierarchies are established by ritualised aggressive
encounters involving grass-pulling with the forepaws. Mobs of 30-50 have large
stable home ranges of up to 100 ha or more abutting those of neighbouring mobs.
Individuals or small groups have overlapping home ranges within this area. When
alarmed they scatter erratically, thumping the ground with the hindfeet as they hop
at high speed with the back and tail almost horizontal. Vocalisations include
submissive coughs, soft clucking during courtship and threatening, growling hisses.
Development. Females mate at 2 years, males at 2-3 years. Births occur throughout
the year with a peak from March to July. They mate near the end of the young's
pouch life, although the embryo remains dormant until the pouch is empty. After a
pregnancy of 34-38 days the single young attaches firmly to one of the four teats in
the mother's pouch. It vacates the pouch at about 39 weeks and suckles at foot until
about 14 months old.
Food. Native grasses, herbs and ferns, seldom drinking.
Habitat. Open forest with a grassy understorey, often in hilly areas.
Status. Common.

Macropus dorsalis

Macropus parryi

Macropus robustus

COMMON WALLAROO

Also known as the Euro, this large marsupial has coarse shaggy
fur, generally dark grey-black above in eastern animals,
reddish-brown in the west, and paler below. Females are
bluish-grey and males may have a reddish band across the
shoulders and neck. The base of the ear, the forelimbs
and tail may be orange. The nose is naked, the tail
short and thick, and the limbs relatively short. The
hindfeet have no first digit, the second and third are
fused with a double claw, and the fourth is much longer
than the others.
Size. Head-body: 570-1085 mm. Tail: 530-900 mm. **Weight**: males to
60 kg, females to 25 kg.
Behaviour. Nocturnal, they rest in caves, under rock ledges or among dense trees,
often above their feeding grounds. They remain in a small overlapping home
ranges, form small impermanent groups varying in size and composition, and are
often solitary. Males rub their chest gland over low vegetation during courtship,
and fight over females in oestrous, with ritualised boxing matches, probably
establishing dominance hierarchies. They make threatening hisses, clucking alarm
calls, and thump the ground with their hindfeet when alarmed.
Development. Sexually mature at 14-24 months, they may live to 15 years. They
breed at any time of year, mating soon after birth, although the embryo remains
dormant until the pouch is vacated. After a pregnancy of 32-34 days the newborn
attaches firmly to one of four teats in the mother's pouch, which it vacates at about
36 weeks, suckling at foot until about 16 months old.
Food. Native grasses and some shrubs. They can survive without drinking.
Habitat. Rocky hills, escarpments and rugged sites.
Status. Common.

Macropus giganteus

EASTERN GREY KANGAROO

A large robust marsupial, this species has soft deep fur varying
from light silver-grey to dark grey flecked with light grey
above, usually paler below. Females have a white chest.
The forehead is grey. The paws, feet and tail tip are
dark grey to black. The nose is hairy. The hindfeet have
no first digit, the second and third are fused with a
double claw, the fourth is much longer than the others.
Size. Head-body: 950-2300 mm. Tail: 430-1090 mm.
Weight: males to 95 kg, females to 40 kg.
Behaviour. Predominantly nocturnal, they rest in the shade and
feed from dusk to dawn, often in mobs of 10 or more, with overlapping
home ranges up to two square kilometres. Males establish dominance hierarchies
by fighting and ritualised acts including grass-pulling with the forefeet. They range
widely searching for females in oestrous. Females usually congregate with female
relatives and will only mate with dominant males. Old males are usually solitary.
When alarmed they make guttural coughs and thump their hindfeet as they hop
away with the body erect and the tail curved up. They will also swim to avoid
predators.
Development. Females mate at 18 months, males at 2 years, and live 10-12 years.
They breed year round with a peak of births in summer. Females mate about 11
days after the pouch is vacated, or in good seasons when the pouch young is more
than 4 months old (the embryo remaining dormant until the pouch is vacated).
After a pregnancy of 33-38 days the newborn attaches firmly to one of four teats in
the mother's pouch, which it vacates at about 11 months, suckling at foot until 18
months old. Twins have been recorded.
Food. Native grasses and shrubs.
Habitat. Dry sclerophyll forests, woodlands and low open scrub.
Status. Common. Subspecies: *M. g. giganteus* mainland; *M. g. tasmaniensis*
Tasmania.

Macropus robustus

Macropus giganteus

Macropus fuliginosus WESTERN GREY KANGAROO

Similar to the Eastern Grey Kangaroo, this species has light to dark chocolate-brown fur often with flecks of grey above, dark brown to black paws, feet and tail tip, and buff patches on the legs and forearms. They are usually paler below. The nose is hairy, the ears are large and fringed with white hairs. The hindfeet have no first digit, the second and third are fused with a double claw, and the fourth is much longer than the others.

Size. Head-body: 950-2225 mm. Tail: 425-1000 mm.
Weight: Males to 72 kg, females to 39 kg.
Behaviour. Nocturnal, they rest in the shelter of trees and shrubs. Subgroups of 2-4 animals have overlapping home ranges of up to 8 square kilometres and belong to a larger mob of 40-50 with a discrete territory. Males have a strong distinctive odour and establish dominance hierarchies by fighting and ritualised acts. They range widely searching for females in oestrous. Females usually congregate with female relatives, form their own dominance hierarchies and and will only mate with dominant males. Old males are usually solitary. When alarmed they make guttural coughs and thump their hindfeet as they hop away with the body erect and the tail curved up.
Development. Females are sexually mature at 16 months, males at 31 months. They breed at any time with a peak of births from September to March. Females mate 2-10 days after the pouch is vacated. After a pregnancy of 28-35 days the single newborn attaches firmly to one of four teats in the mother's pouch, which it vacates at about 10 months, suckling at foot until 18 months old.
Food. Native grasses.
Habitat. Open forests, woodlands and open scrub.
Status. Common.

Macropus rufus RED KANGAROO

One of the largest living marsupials and powerfully built, the Red Kangaroo is reddish-brown above and paler below, although eastern females are blue-grey. A broad white stripe runs along the cheek, the muzzle has black and white markings with a partially naked tip. The hindfeet have no first digit, the second and third are fused with a double claw, and the fourth is much longer than the others.
Size. Head-body: 745-1400 mm. Tail: 645-1000 mm.
Weight: males to 95 kg, females to 37 kg. Males are very broad and muscular.
Behaviour. Active mainly at night, they also feed on cool wet days, and rest in dusty scrapes under bushes or shrubs. Groups of 2-10 occupy a home range of around 8 square kilometres. This area increases in droughts when mobs of several hundred may gather around scarce resources. Males congregate around females in oestrous and establish dominance hierarchies by boxing. The largest males have exclusive mating rights. Young males range widely and old males become solitary. When alarmed they make a loud cough and thump their hindfeet, hopping rapidly away with the body and tail horizontal.
Development. Males are sexually mature at 2-3 years, females at 15-20 months. In good years they breed all year round, mating soon after birth, the embryo remaining dormant until the pouch is vacated. After a pregnancy of 32-34 days the newborn attaches firmly to one of four teats in the mother's pouch, which it vacates by 9 months, suckling at foot for another 3 months. They may live 20 years.
Food. Native grasses, herbs. Can survive without water if the food is green.
Habitat. Dry woodlands, scrub, grasslands, plains and deserts.
Status. Common.

Macropus fuliginosus

Macropus rufus

Pteropus poliocephalus   GREY-HEADED FLYING-FOX

A winged placental mammal with long fur, dark brown above and grey below often flecked with white or yellow-brown. The fox-like head is light grey with a reddish brown mantle encircling the neck. Thick leg fur extends to the ankle. They moult in June, having darker winter fur. The eyes are large, the ears simple, and they lack a tail. Both first and second fingers are clawed.
Size. Head-body: 230-280 mm. Forearm: 138-164 mm.
Weight. 0.46-1.05 kg. Males are larger than females.
Behaviour. Active mainly at night, they roost in large trees, hanging from their feet with the head pointing forward and the wings wrapped around the body. Camps of up to 5,000 form in summer. Males use secretions of their shoulder glands to attract females and mark territories which they defend by fighting, slapping their folded wings against their sides and shrieking. Young adults and older males move to the periphery of the camp and keep guard. Pregnant females form separate maternity camps in September and are rejoined by the males after giving birth. In the south the juveniles form winter camps with a few adults. Others disperse to live alone or in small nomadic groups. They navigate by sight and avoid complete darkness.
Development. Sexually mature at 18 months, they mate in March and April. A single young is born in September and October and suckles from a teat in the mother's armpit, clinging to her fur and carried for 3-4 weeks until well-furred. They are then left in the camp at night. They can fly at 8-10 weeks and are independent by 4 months.
Food. Eucalypt blossom and nectar, fruits. They can drink seawater.
Habitat. Wet and dry sclerophyll forests, mangroves.
Status. Common.

Pteropus scapulatus   LITTLE RED FLYING-FOX

With a wingspan of about 1 m, this winged placental mammal has soft, short, dense fur, reddish-brown to yellowish-brown above and paler below with a light brown to yellow collar encircling the neck, patches of creamy-brown where the wings meet the shoulders, pale yellow hairs on the underside of the translucent wing membranes, and naked legs. The fox-like head has large eyes and simple ears. They have no tail. The first two fingers have claws.
Size. Head-body: 195-235 mm. Forearm: 120-145 mm.
Weight. 200-605 g. Males are larger than females.
Behaviour. Active at night on and overcast afternoons, they roost in trees, hanging by their feet with the head pointing forward and the wings wrapped around the body. Camps of up to one million (depending on food supply) form in November and December. Male-female pairs establish territories marked by secretions of the male's shoulder gland, and juveniles form their own groups in the camps. Females form separate groups after mating, establish new camps, or join those of other flying-foxes. Camps disperse around February. They are highly nomadic, travelling long distances searching for blossoming trees. They navigate by sight, avoiding total darkness. Columns of bats are often seen leaving the camps at dusk.
Development. Sexually mature at 18 months, they mate in December and January. A single young is born in April or May and suckles from a teat in the mother's armpit. Young are carried until well-furred, then left at the roost at night.
Food. Eucalypt blossom and nectar, fruits.
Habitat. Rainforests, sclerophyll forests and woodlands.
Status. Common.

Pteropus poliocephalus

Pteropus scapulatus

Pteropus alecto

This winged placental mammal has soft fur, dark brown to black above, often flecked with grey below and sometimes reddish-brown on the shoulders and the back of the neck. The fox-like head has large eyes and simple ears. They have no tail. The first and second fingers are clawed. The five toes have long curved claws.
Size. Head-body: 240-300 mm. Forearm: 138-185 mm.
Weight. 280-760 g. Males are larger than females.
Behaviour. Active mainly at night, they navigate by sight and avoid flying in total darkness. They roost by day in the branches of large trees, hanging upside down by their feet with the head pointing forward and the wings wrapped around the body. Camps form in September and October and may comprise hundreds of thousands of bats, often including Grey-headed and Little Red Flying-foxes. Males establish territories along branches about 1 m across, scent-marked by their shoulder glands. Camps decline in April at the end of the breeding season. Most bats disperse in winter and live alone or in small groups, a few remain in the camps. They fly with rapid wing beats at 35-40 kph.
Development. Mating takes place in March and April. A single young is born from August to November and suckles from a teat in the mother's armpit. Clinging with the feet it is carried for 3-4 weeks until well-furred, then left in the camp at night. They can fly at 2 months and are independent at about 13 weeks.
Food. Blossoms and fruits. They can drink seawater.
Habitat. Rainforests, mangroves, wet sclerophyll forests.
Status. Common. Also found in eastern Indonesia and New Guinea.

Pteropus conspicillatus

This winged placental mammal is an essential pollinator and distributor of rainforest plants. It has soft dense fur, dark brown to black, often flecked with white above. Pale yellow areas around the eyes usually extend to the snout. They have a yellow collar partially encircling the neck, a fox-like head with large eyes and simple ears, and lack a tail. Both first and second fingers are clawed, and the five toes have long curved claws.
Size. Head-body: 220-240 mm. Forearm: 155-175 mm.
Weight. 350-600 g. Males are larger than females.
Behaviour. Active mainly at night, they navigate by sight and avoid flying in total darkness. They roost in the branches of large trees, hanging upside down by their feet, the head pointing forward and the wings wrapped around the body. Coastal camps are often continually occupied and may comprise many thousands of bats. Males mark territories and attract females during the mating season by secretions of their shoulder glands. In winter and summer many join highland camps where food is more plentiful. Pregnant females form highland maternity camps in summer. No more than two bats feed in a tree, which they defend by chasing away intruders, shrieking, and slapping their folded wings against the sides of the body.
Development. Sexually mature at 2 years, they mate from March to May and give birth to a single young from October to December. Newborn suckle from a teat in the mother's armpit and are carried for 1-2 weeks until well-furred. They are then left in the camp at night and become independent at about 12 weeks.
Food. Blossom and fruits. They drink seawater while skimming over the surface.
Habitat. Rainforests, mangroves and wet sclerophyll forests.
Status. Common. Also found in New Guinea and surrounding islands.

Pteropus alecto

Pteropus conspicillatus

Syconycteris australis
QUEENSLAND BLOSSOM-BAT

A small bat and an important pollinator in the tropics, this winged placental mammal feeds on nectar. It has a long, thin, brush-like tongue and a slim, pointed muzzle. The long soft fur extends to the ankle. It is reddish-brown to fawn above, paler below and flecked with white. The head is fox-like with simple rounded ears. They lack a tail, have a large claw on the first finger and a tiny claw on the second finger. The incisor teeth are slender and weak.

Size. Head-body: 40-50Tmm. Forearm: 38-43 mm. **Weight.** 13-19 g. Males are larger than females.

Behaviour. Active mainly at night, they roost by day alone or in small groups in dense foliage such as tangled vines and mango trees, hanging upside down with the wings wrapped around the body. When feeding they hover over a selected blossom and repeatedly slap the sides of the body with their wings to establish a feeding territory and deter any intruders. They have an acute sense of smell and good vision. They navigate by sight and avoid flying in total darkness. They fly 3-5 m above the ground and often follow tracks through the forest to feeding sites.

Development. Little is known about their development. They may breed more than once a year, giving birth to a single young which suckles from a teat in the mother's armpit and is carried with her until well-furred.

Food. Nectar and pollen of banksias, paperbarks, bottlebrushes, bananas and other flowering trees and shrubs.

Habitat. Rainforests and wet sclerophyll forests.

Status. Common.

Nyctimene robinsoni
QUEENSLAND TUBE-NOSED BAT

This distinctive winged placental mammal is characterised by its prominent tubular nostrils which extend from the muzzle by 5-6 mm, and by the pale yellow-green spots on the wings and ears. The fur is long and soft, grey-brown to light brown above and paler below, usually with a dark brown stripe along the centre of the back. It has simple rounded ears, a short free tail and claws on both first and second fingers.

Size. Head-body: 100-110 mm. Tail: 20-25 mm. Forearm: 60-70 mm. **Weight.** 30-50 g. Males are larger than females.

Behaviour. Active mainly at night, they roost alone in trees close to their feeding sites hanging from a branch with the head pointing forward and the wings wrapped around the body. Some change roosts daily, depending on the food supply. Nomadic and aggressive, they sometimes form large feeding groups around fruiting trees, probably defending feeding territories. They have good vision and avoid flying in total darkness. They forage in the forest understorey, flying close to the ground along forest tracks, often making whistling calls.

Development. Little is known about their development. They give birth to a single young between October and December which suckles from a teat in the mother's armpit and is carried with her until well-furred.

Food. Fruits, particularly those of trunk-fruiting trees, nectar and pollen. They can survive without drinking.

Habitat. Rainforest, wet and dry sclerophyll forests and woodlands.

Status. Common.

Syconycteris australis

Nyctimene robinsoni

Macroderma gigas

Also known as the False Vampire Bat, this carnivorous winged
placental mammal has long soft fur, fawn-grey to dove-grey
above and pale grey to white below. The ears are very
large, joined above the head and sparsely-haired with a
forked lobe partially covering the aperture. They have
no tail. The eyes are large and a simple large noseleaf
projects above the snout.
Size. Head-body: 100-130 mm. Forearm: 102-112 mm.
Weight. 100-165 g.
Behaviour. Active mainly at night, they roost in deep caves, rock
fissures and mines, at least 2 m above the floor, and form colonies
of up to 400 in the summer breeding season. Males and females often occupy
separate caves after mating. Pregnant females congregate in the warmest caves in
early spring, sometimes shifting their young to nursing caves. The whole colony
reassembles in the warmest caves in early winter and disperses in July. They fly
smooth and straight with the head held high, orienting by sight and by intermittent
use of echo-location, emitting signals through the mouth. They locate prey visually
and by sound while sitting on a branch. Small terrestrial animals are killed by
enveloping them in their wings and biting them to death. Other bats may be caught
in flight. They feed at their roost or perch.
Development. Mating from April to August, a single young is born from September
to November and suckles from a teat in the mother's armpit. It is carried until well-
furred at 4 weeks, and then left in the roost until able to fly by 7 weeks.
Food. Insects, birds, lizards, frogs, mice, bats and other vertebrates.
Habitat. Rainforests, wet and dry sclerophyll forests and arid woodlands.
Status. Sparse. Subspecies: *M. g. saturata* Pilbara region, W.A.; *M. g. gigas* elsewhere.

Macroglossus minimus

A small bat and an important pollinator of paperbark trees, this
winged placental mammal has a long, narrow, bristly tongue
used to probe into flowers for nectar and pollen. The
long soft fur is fawn to reddish-brown above and paler
below, and extends to the ankles. The head is fox-like
with a tapering muzzle and simple, broad, rounded ears.
The tail is small and rudimentary. There is a large
claw on the first finger and a tiny claw on the second
finger. The incisor teeth are slender, weak, and often malformed.
Size. Head-body: 59-64 mm. Forearm: 37-42 mm. **Weight**. 11-19 g.
Males are larger than females.
Behaviour. Active mainly at night, they roost by day alone or in small groups in the
branches of trees, under loose bark, in rolled banana leaves and buildings. They
hang upside down with the wings wrapped around the body. When feeding they
can hover beside blossoms and probe with the tongue. They have an acute sense of
smell, navigate by sight, and avoid flying in total darkness.
Development. Little is known about their development. They are known to give
birth to a single young in the dry season (August to September), although the
breeding season may be much longer than this. Females have a single teat under
each armpit from which the newborn suckles, gripping onto her fur with its clawed
feet and being carried around until well-furred.
Food. Nectar and pollen of a variety of trees.
Habitat. Rainforests, mangroves, paperbark and bamboo thickets, banana
plantations and monsoon scrub.
Status. Common. Widespread in southeast Asia.

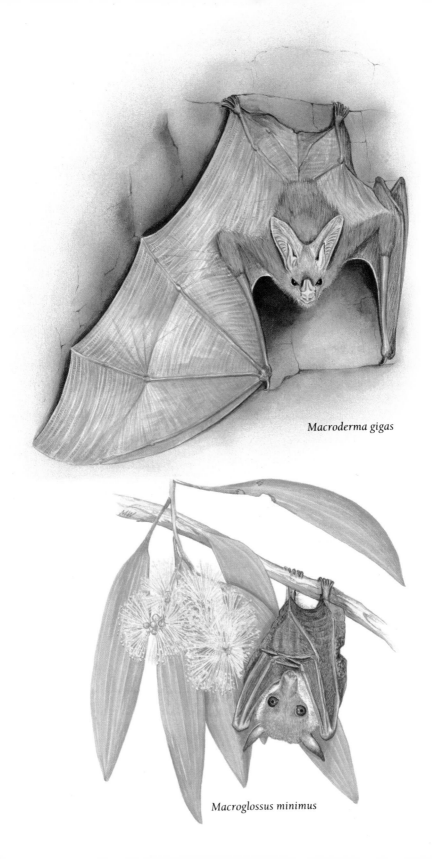

Macroderma gigas

Macroglossus minimus

Rhinonycteris aurantius ORANGE HORSESHOE-BAT

A small, variously-coloured insectivorous winged placental mammal,
this species is bright orange to greyish-brown, sometimes
pale lemon or white above (depending on the locality),
often with dark bands across the eyes. The ears are
sharply pointed and the eyes are small. A complex
noseleaf lies above the snout with a horseshoe-shaped
indented lower part, a scalloped upper section with
deep pits and a forward projection in the centre. The
tail protrudes slightly beyond the tail membrane.
Size. Head-body: 45-56 mm. Tail: 24-28 mm. Forearm: 45-51 mm.
Weight. 7-10 g. Males are larger than females.
Behaviour. Active mainly at night, they roost in deep, warm, humid caves usually
with difficult access to avoid predators such as the Ghost Bat, and change caves on
a regular seasonal basis. They hang from the roof with the head hanging down, or
rest against a wall with the forearms spread well apart, forming colonies of 20 to
12,000 or more, roosting some 150 mm apart with the wings wrapped around the
body. They have good sight and can detect prey up to 2 m away using echo-
location, emitting ultrasonic signals through the nose and directing them with the
noseleaf. Their broad wings enable them to fly slowly through the forest
understorey and lower canopy hunting for insects.
Development. Little studied, they are thought to mate from October to April.
Females give birth to a single young which suckles from a teat in her armpit. **Food.**
Insects caught on the wing or gleaned from the foliage.
Habitat. Mangroves, spinifex grasslands, vine thickets, dense palm forests and
woodlands.
Status. Sparse.

Hipposideros ater DUSKY HORSESHOE-BAT

A small insectivorous winged placental mammal, this species has
long soft fur, light grey above tipped with blackish-brown
to orange, and slightly paler below. The ears are very
large and broad with a slight point. The eyes are small,
and a simple noseleaf with a horseshoe-shaped lower
ridge projects above the snout. The tail protrudes
slightly beyond the tail membrane.
Size. Head-body: 40-50 mm. Tail: 20-30 mm.
Forearm: 37-41 mm. **Weight.** 8-10 g.
Behaviour. Active mainly at night, they roost by day in caves,
crevices and mines, hanging from the roof with the wings wrapped
around the body and the head hanging down. Both sexes share roosts without
territoriality or segregation. They form colonies during the summer breeding
season, and many disperse during the winter. They often feed in small groups,
returning to the cave entrance to digest their food before leaving to forage again.
They have good sight, and ultrasonic signals emitted through the nose and directed
by the noseleaf allow them to echo-locate their prey and navigate. They have broad
wings and fly slowly through the forest understorey.
Development. They mate in April and give birth to a single young in October or
November. Females have two false teats in the pubic region and one functioning
teat under each armpit from which the newborn suckles until December or January.
Food. Flying insects caught on the wing.
Habitat. Rainforests, open forests and dry vine thickets.
Status. Sparse. Widespread in New Guinea. Subspecies: *H. a. albanensis* northern
Qld; *H. a. gilberti* Kimberleys and N.T.

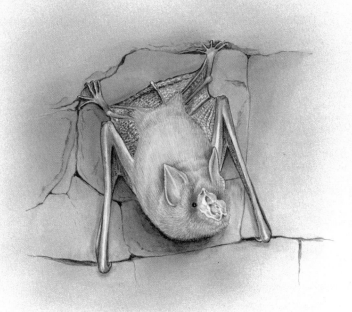

Rhinonycteris aurantius

Hipposideros ater

Rhinolophus megaphyllus EASTERN HORSESHOE-BAT

A small insectivorous winged placental mammal, this bat has long,
soft, greyish-brown fur. Some northern animals are orange-
brown. The ears are large, simple and sharply-pointed. The
eyes are very small. There is a complex complex noseleaf
above the snout with a horseshoe-shaped lower part, a
scalloped upper section and a fleshy central projection.
The tail does not protrude beyond the tail membrane.
Size. Head-body: 40-60 mm. Tail: 35-45 mm.
Forearm: 44-50 mm. **Weight**. 9-14 g.
Behaviour. Active mainly at night, they roost by day in humid
caves, mines and buildings, hanging from the roof 15-20 cm apart
with the feet together, the head hanging down and the wings wrapped around the
body. Colonies exceeding 1,000 bats gather in large caves. Adult females disperse
in September and October to form maternity colonies. They have good vision and
echo-locate their prey, emitting high-pitched sounds through the nose and directing
them with the noseleaf. They fly slowly or hover, alighting in small bushes 1-2 m
high, rotating back and forth and making short flights every few minutes to catch
insects. Aquatic insects are taken from the surface of water.
Development. Males are sexually mature at 2 years, females at 2-3 years. They
mate from April to June and give birth to a single young from October to December.
Females have two false teats in the pubic area and one functional teat under each
armpit from which the newborn suckles. Young are carried clinging to her false
teats and fur until well-furred. They are then left clustered in a maternity cave
while she forages, and are weaned at 2 months.
Food. Large flying and aquatic insects.
Habitat. Rainforests, open coastal scrub and tall forests.
Status. Common in the north, sparse in the south. Subspecies: *R. m. magaphyllus*
north of Bramston Beach in Qld; *R. m. ignifer* southern areas.

Taphozous georgianus COMMON SHEATHTAIL-BAT

A widespread insectivorous winged placental mammal, the Common
Sheathtail-bat has dark brown fur with a creamy-white base
above. It is light brown below flecked with grey under
the arms. There are sparse yellow hairs under the base
of the tail. Both sexes have wing pockets of unknown
function below the wrists. The tail protrudes through
the tail-membrane and slides freely, increasing hindlimb
movement. The face is dog-like with large ridged ears
and a prominent lobe partially covering the ear aperture.
Size. Head-body: 65-85 mm. Tail: 25-35 mm. Forearm: 65-75 mm.
Weight. 17-51 g (depending on the amount of body fat accumulated).
Behaviour. Active at night, they roost with up to 100 others, well-spaced, in caves,
rock fissures and mine shafts in the twilight zone, clinging crab-like to the walls.
They cluster together in cold conditions and become torpid. When disturbed they
scuttle quickly around the walls and hide in crevices. They relocate regularly and
may form maternity colonies. Their vision is good. They emit high-pitched sounds
through the mouth and echo-locating insects up to 10 m away while flying high and
fast, often following a grid pattern.
Development. Females are sexually mature at 9 months, males at 21 months. They
mate from late August to September and give birth to a single young from
November to December. Newborn suckle from a teat in the mother's armpit and
are carried until independent at 18-33 days. They live to 5 years or more.
Food. Beetles and other flying insects.
Habitat. Wet and dry sclerophyll forests and woodlands.
Status. Common and widespread.

Rhinolophus megaphyllus

Taphozous georgianus

Taphozous hilli

HILL'S SHEATHTAIL-BAT

Often found roosting with the Common Sheathtail-bat (*T. georgianus*), Hill's Sheathtail-bat is a slightly different colour and the males have a small throat pouch. The fur is rich clove-brown fur above and grades to light brown on the rump. Belly fur is light buff tipped with olive-brown. The wings are greyish-brown. The forearms are curved and lack wing pockets. The tail protrudes through the tail-membrane and slides freely, allowing increased hindlimb movement. The face is dog-like with large ridged ears with a prominent lobe partially covering the ear aperture.
Size. Head-body: 63-75 mm. Tail: 25-35 mm. Forearm: 63-72 mm.
Weight. 20-25 g.
Behaviour. Active at night, they roost in small colonies of up to 25 in caves, rock fissures and mine shafts in the twilight zone, clinging crab-like to the walls. When disturbed they scuttle quickly around the walls and hide in crevices. They have good vision and detect insects by echo-location, emitting high-pitched sounds through the mouth while flying quickly above and around trees.
Development. Little is known about their development. Females give birth to a single young between December and April. Newborn suckle from a teat in the mother's armpit.
Food. Insects.
Habitat. Arid and semi-arid woodlands in rocky, hilly country.
Status. Common to sparse.

Saccolaimus flaviventris

YELLOW-BELLIED SHEATHTAIL-BAT

The largest Australian sheathtail-bat, this winged placental mammal is easily distinguished by its contrasting glossy black back and white or creamy-yellow belly. Both sexes have a throat pouch which is well-developed in males and reduced to a rudimentary fold of skin in females. The wings are long and narrow with the tips folded back over the membrane at rest, and lack wing pockets. The tip of the tail is covered with bristles and protrudes through the tail-membrane, sliding freely to increase hindlimb movement. The face is dog-like, mostly naked, with black skin and thick, leathery, ribbed ears with a prominent lobe partially covering the ear aperture.
Size. Head-body: 75-90 mm. Tail: 20-35 mm. Forearm: 72-80 mm.
Weight. 30-60 g.
Behaviour. Active at night, they roost alone or with up to 10 others in large hollow trees, the abandoned nests of Sugar Gliders or in buildings. They are good climbers and fly fast direct with slow wing beats, hunting high above the forest canopy and in forest clearings. They have good vision and detect insects by echo-location, emitting audible calls through the mouth while flying.
Development. Nothing is known about their reproduction and development.
Food. Flying insects, particularly beetles and moths.
Habitat. Rainforests, sclerophyll forests and woodlands.
Status. Common in the tropics, sparse elsewhere, possibly underestimated.

Taphozous hilli

Saccolaimus flaviventris

Nyctinomus australis

WHITE-STRIPED MASTIFF-BAT

Although fierce-looking, this winged placental mammal is quite docile and derives its name from the upturned hound-like snout. The fur is short and dense, chocolate-brown to reddish-brown or black above. It is paler below with white stripes along the junction of the wings and body, and sometimes has white patches on the chest. The ears are fleshy, rounded, almost touching above the head and strongly ribbed. The upper lip is deeply wrinkled. Both sexes have a deep wide throat pouch of unknown function. The toes are thick, fleshy and fringed with long, stiff, curved hairs. The tail projects well beyond the tail-membrane.

Size. Head-body: 85-100 mm. Tail: 40-55 mm. Forearm: 55-65 mm.
Weight. 25-40 g.
Behaviour. Active at night, they roost alone or in small colonies of less than 20 bats in tree hollows, under bark and in buildings. They are fast fliers but have difficulty taking off from the ground, and usually crawl onto a rock or tree to launch themselves. They hunt above the canopy, have good sight, and detect insects by echo-location, emitting high-pitched, metallic-sounding calls from the mouth. They also forage on the ground, scurrying around searching for terrestrial insects.
Development. Little is known about their development. A single young is born in November or December and suckles from a teat in the mother's armpit.
Food. Insects.
Habitat. Wet and dry sclerophyll forests, arid woodlands and urban areas.
Status. Locally common but sparse in the central desert. Subspecies: *T. a. australis* most of the range; *T. a. atratus* central desert.

Mormopterus planiceps

LITTLE MASTIFF-BAT

A small insectivorous bat with an upturned, hound-like snout, this winged placental mammal has a flattened head and body enabling it to hide in small cracks and crevices. The soft fur is grey to brownish-grey above and paler below. Two subspecies appear to exist. The northern subspecies has shorter fur and males have a penis less than 5 mm long. The southern subspecies has shaggier, longer fur and the male penis is longer than than 9 mm. The large triangular ears are not joined above the head. The protruding, wrinkled upper lip has a dense fringe of stiff hairs. The feet are stout with fleshy toes fringed with stiff curled hairs. The tail projects well beyond the tail-membrane.

Size. Head-body: 50-65 mm. Tail: 30-40 mm. Forearm: 30-40 mm.
Weight. 9-15 g.
Behaviour. Active mainly at night, they roost by day alone or in colonies of up to 100 bats in tree hollows and crevices, under loose bark and in buildings. They are docile to handle but aggressive to other bats, although they often share roosts with other species. They fly fast and direct above the forest canopy, have good sight, and detect insects by echo-location, emitting high-pitched audible calls from the mouth. They forage over creeks and waterholes and on the ground, scurrying around searching for terrestrial insects. They can swim well if necessary.
Development. Little is known about their development. A single young is born in December and suckles from a teat in the mother's armpit.
Food. Flying and terrestrial insects.
Habitat. Dry sclerophyll forests, woodlands and deserts.
Status. Common.

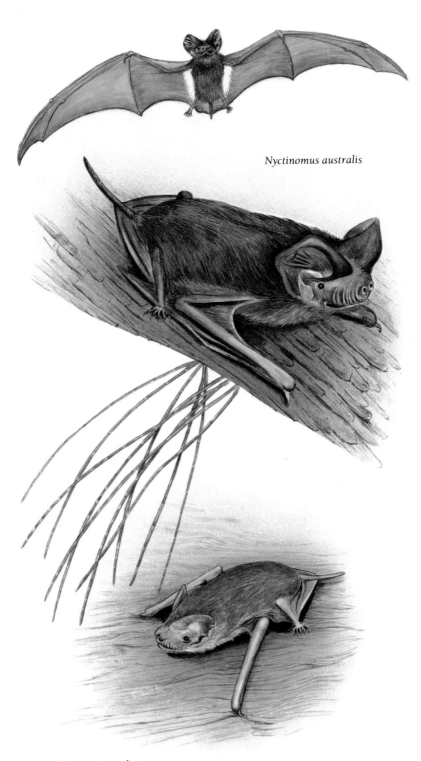

Nyctinomus australis

Mormopterus planiceps

Mormopterus norfolkensis
EASTERN LITTLE MASTIFF-BAT

Also known as the Norfolk Island Mastiff-bat, this tiny winged placental mammal was mistakenly assumed to come from Norfolk Island. The upturned snout and protruding wrinkled upper lip give it a bulldog-like appearance. The soft fur is dark brownish-grey to reddish-brown above and slightly paler below. The large triangular ears are not joined above the head. Males have a neck pouch of unknown function. The feet have thick fleshy toes fringed with long, stiff, curled hairs. The tail projects well beyond the tail-membrane.

Size. Head-body: 45-55 mm. Tail: 30-40 mm. Forearm: 35-40 mm.
Weight. 6-10 g.
Behaviour. Active mainly at night, they roost by day alone or in small colonies in tree hollows and crevices, under loose bark, in caves and buildings. They fly fast and direct with limited manoeuvrability above the forest canopy and clearings. They have good sight, and detect insects by echo-location, emitting high-pitched calls from the mouth. They also forage on the ground, scurrying around searching for terrestrial insects.
Development. Their development has not been studied. They probably give birth to a single young that suckles from a teat in the mother's armpit.
Food. Flying and terrestrial insects.
Habitat. Wet sclerophyll forests and woodlands.
Status. Sparse.

Mormopterus beccarii
BECCARI'S MASTIFF-BAT

Often confused with the Little Mastiff-bat (*M. planiceps*) this species is larger and found in the northeastern part of Australia. A small insectivorous bat with a bull-dog appearance, this winged placental mammal has a large wrinkled upper lip with a fringe of stiff hairs and furrowed cheeks. It has a flattened head and body and hides in small cracks and crevices. The soft fur is dark grey-brown above and paler below. The large triangular ears are not joined above the head. The feet are stout with fleshy toes fringed with stiff curled hairs. The tail projects well beyond the tail-membrane.

Size. Head-body: 55-65 mm. Tail: 27-35 mm. Forearm: 35-41 mm.
Weight. 13-19 g.
Behaviour. Active mainly at night, they roost by day in colonies of up to 50 bats in tree hollows and crevices, under loose bark and in buildings. They fly fast and direct above the forest canopy and over water, hunting their prey by echo-location, emitting high-pitched calls from the mouth, enabling them to detect insects up to 10 m away. They have good sight and can crawl rapidly on the ground.
Development. Little is known about their development. A single young is born in November, suckles from a teat in the mother's armpit, and is weaned in January.
Food. Flying insects.
Habitat. Wet and dry sclerophyll forests, woodlands and urban areas.
Status. Common and widespread. Also found from East Indonesia to Melanesia.

Mormopterus norfolkensis

Mormopterus beccarii

Nyctophilus geoffroyi LESSER LONG-EARED BAT

Found in most parts of Australia, this tiny insectivorous winged placental mammal has long fluffy fur, light grey-brown above and paler below. The eyes are small, the long ears are joined above the head and ribbed, with a short lower lobe. A small low noseleaf with a central Y-shaped groove projects above the snout. The tail is enclosed in the tail-membrane.

Size. Head-body: 40-50 mm. Tail: 20-25 mm. Forearm: 30-45 mm. **Weight**. 4-13 g.

Behaviour. Active mainly at night, they roost alone or in colonies of up to 200 or more in tree hollows, caves, abandoned bird nests, under loose bark, under rocks and in buildings, usually clinging to a wall with the head hanging down. Maternity colonies form in spring, and may include adult males in some locations. They disperse in autumn when the young are independent. In southern areas they hibernate through winter or become torpid during the day. They fly slowly with high manoeuvrability and can lift off vertically from the ground, foraging in the understorey, hovering over leaves and landing to take flightless insects. They have good vision and use echo-location to navigate and detect insects at short distances.

Development. Males produce sperm in summer and store it until mating in autumn. Females store this sperm through the winter, fertilising their ova in early spring and giving birth usually to twins from September to November. Newborn suckle from teats in the mother's armpits and are carried until well-furred. They are then left at the roost while the mother forages, and are weaned at 6-8 weeks.

Food. Flying and terrestrial insects.

Habitat. All habitats except tropical and subtropical rainforests.

Status. Common. Subspecies: *N. g. geoffroyi* W.A.; *N. g. pallescens* northern S.A.; *N. g. pacificus* eastern Australia and Tasmania.

Mormopterus loriae LITTLE NORTHERN MASTIFF-BAT

A tiny insectivorous bat with an upturned, hound-like snout, this winged placental mammal is flattened from the side enabling it to hide in small cracks and crevices. The soft fur is light brownish-grey with a whitish base both above and below. The large rounded ears are not joined above the head. The protruding wrinkled upper lip has a dense fringe of stiff hairs. Males have a neck pouch of unknown function. The feet are stout with fleshy toes fringed with stiff curled hairs. The tail projects well beyond the tail-membrane.

Size. Head-body: 40-55 mm. Tail: 25-40 mm. Forearm: 28-35 mm. **Weight**. 6-10 g.

Behaviour. Active mainly at night, they roost by day alone or in colonies of several hundred bats in tree hollows and crevices, under loose bark, in caves and buildings. They fly fast and direct with limited manoeuvrability above the forest canopy. They have good sight and detect insects by echo-location, emitting high-pitched calls from the mouth. They also forage over creeks and waterholes and on the ground, scurrying around searching for terrestrial insects.

Development. Little is known about their development. A single young is born in October or November and suckles from a teat in the mother's armpit, until weaned about one month later.

Food. Flying and terrestrial insects.

Habitat. Dry sclerophyll forests and woodlands.

Status. Common. Extends to New Guinea. Subspecies: *M. l. coburgensis* N.T.; *M. l. ridei* east coast.

Nyctophilus geoffroyi

Mormopterus loriae

Nyctophilus gouldi

A small insectivorous winged placental mammal, Gould's Long-eared
Bat is slate grey to grey-brown above and ash-grey below
mottled with light buff. The eyes are small. The long
ears are joined above the head and ribbed, with a
short, broad, triangular lower lobe partially covering
the aperture. A poorly-developed noseleaf forms a well
defined ridge behind the nostrils. The tail is enclosed
in the tail-membrane.
Size. Head-body: 50-65 mm. Tail: 45-55 mm.
Forearm: 35-45 mm. **Weight.** 6-14 g.
Behaviour. Active mainly at night, they roost alone or in colonies
of up to 25 in tree hollows, under loose bark, in abandoned bird nests and
buildings. They prefer trees greater than 800 mm diameter, and change roosts
almost daily within a group of trees, staying in the same district. In southern areas
and semi-arid regions they hibernate through winter. Their broad wings allow them
to fly slowly with high manoeuvrability. They usually stay within 2 km of the roost,
foraging in the understorey for flying insects, and gleaning flightless insects from
foliage. They have good vision and use echo-location to navigate and detect insects.
Development. Females are sexually active at 7-9 months, males at 12-15 months.
Males produce sperm in summer and store it until mating in autumn. Females store
this sperm through the winter, fertilise their ova in early spring and give birth to
1-2 young in late October or November. Newborn suckle from teats in the mother's
armpits and are carried until weaned at about 6 weeks.
Food. Insects.
Habitat. Wet and dry sclerophyll forests and woodlands, favouring higher rainfall
areas.
Status. Common.

Nyctophilus bifax

A small winged placental mammal, the Northern Long-eared Bat is
light brown or tawny-brown above and greyish-brown below.
The eyes are relatively large. The head is foreshortened
and has long ribbed ears, each with a short, broadly
triangular lower lobe partially covering the aperture.
A poorly-developed noseleaf forms a low ridge behind
the nostrils. The tail is enclosed in the tail-membrane.
Size. Head-body: 45-55 mm. Tail: 40-45 mm.
Forearm: 32-45 mm. **Weight.** 8-12 g.
Behaviour. Active mainly at night, they roost in tree hollows
and buildings. Their broad wings allow them to fly slowly with high
manoeuvrability and to hover and take off from the ground. They forage in the
understorey for flying insects and glean flightless insects from foliage and the
ground. They usually hang from trees 5-10 m high, rotate back and forth and make
short flights every few minutes to catch insects. They have good vision and use
low-intensity echo-location to navigate and detect insects.
Development. Little is known about their development. Females give birth usually
to twins in mid-summer. Newborn suckle from teats in the mother's armpits.
Food. Insects.
Habitat. Tropical rainforests, woodlands, dry sclerophyll forests and other habitats,
often near watercourses.
Status. Common.

Nyctophilus gouldi

Nyctophilus bifax

Miniopterus schreibersii

One of the world's most widely distributed mammals, the Common Bent-wing Bat is so-called because the exceptionally long terminal segment of the third finger (which supports the tip of the wing membrane) is bent under the wing at rest. The fur is chocolate brown above and paler below. Patches of bright rufous fur appear during the annual moult, and old bats are gingerish. The forehead is high and well-furred, the muzzle short. The tail is enclosed in the tail-membrane and folded under the body at rest.

Size. Head-body: 50-60 mm. Tail: 50-60 mm. Forearm: 45-50 mm. **Weight.** 13-20 g.

Behaviour. Nocturnal, they roost in caves, mine tunnels and buildings, often with *M. australis* in the south, hanging from the roof or walls in closely-massed clusters of the same sex or age group. They use the same roosts every year. Both sexes congregate in spring, and pregnant females from various colonies move to specific maternity roosts up to 250 km away to raise their young, forming colonies of up to 150,000. In February and March they disband and individuals migrate to winter roosts where they hibernate during the coldest months in southern areas. They fly fast and direct, generally hunting above the forest canopy and travelling up to 70 m in one night. They have good vision and use echo-location to navigate and detect insects.

Development. Females are sexually mature in their second year. They mate in September in the north, and May to June in the south (the embryo remaining dormant until close to the end of hibernation in August). A single young is born in late November or December and suckles from a teat in the mother's armpit until weaned in February. They may live to 20 years.

Food. Flying insects.

Habitat. Wet and dry sclerophyll forests and rainforests.

Status. Common. Subspecies: *M. s. oceanensis* east coast; *M. s. orianae* N.T. and Kimberleys.

Miniopterus australis

So-called because the exceptionally long terminal segment of the third finger (which supports the tip of the wing membrane) is bent under the wing at rest, this placental mammal is greyish-black to fawn brown above and paler below. Moulting early in the year, the fur gradually becomes browner. The forehead is high and well-furred, the muzzle short. The tail is enclosed in the tail-membrane and folded under the body at rest.

Size. Head-body: 43-48 mm. Tail: 47-48 mm. Forearm: 36-40 mm. **Weight.** 7-8 g.

Behaviour. Nocturnal, they roost in caves, mine tunnels and buildings, often with *M. screibersii* in the south, hanging from the roof or walls. Colonies of up to 100,000 or more form in early spring. Most of the adult males and juveniles disperse in summer, leaving maternity colonies of females and their young. In winter they occupy cool caves in the south and become torpid. They have good vision and use echo-location to navigate and detect insects, flying relatively slowly and hunting below the forest canopy.

Development. Mating in July or August, a single young is born in December and suckles from a teat in the mother's armpit until weaned in February.

Food. Flying insects.

Habitat. Wet and dry sclerophyll forests and rainforests.

Status. Common. Threatened by mining of nursery caves. Extends to South-East Asia, Indonesia, Melanesia and the Philippines.

Miniopterus schreibersii

Miniopterus australis

Nyctophilus arnhemensis   ARNHEM LAND LONG-EARED BAT

A small, tropical, insectivorous winged placental mammal, the Arnhem Land Long-eared Bat is olive-brown to light brown above and pale brown to greyish-brown below with dark bases to the hair. The eyes are relatively large. The head is foreshortened with long ribbed ears each with a short, broadly-triangular lower lobe. A poorly-developed noseleaf forms a low ridge behind the nostrils. The tail is enclosed in the tail-membrane.

Size. Head-body: 42-55 mm. Tail: 35-43 mm. Forearm: 35-40 mm. **Weight.** 6-8 g.

Behaviour. Active mainly at night, they roost by day in tree hollows, under the loose bark of paperbark trees and in buildings. Their broad wings allow them to fly slowly with high manoeuvrability. They forage in the forest understorey and over water for flying insects, and glean flightless insects from foliage and the ground. They have good vision and use echo-location to navigate and detect insects.

Development. Little is known about their development. Females give birth to 1-2 young from October to February. Newborn suckle from teats in the mother's armpits.

Food. Insects.

Habitat. Tropical rainforests, mangroves, woodlands and wet sclerophyll forests with an annual rainfall exceeding 500 mm.

Status. Common in a limited habitat.

Chalinolobus gouldii   GOULD'S WATTLED BAT

Found in most of Australia, this insectivorous winged placental mammal has soft dense fur, dark chocolate brown to black above, often grading to brown towards the rump, and slightly lighter below. The muzzle is short and the forehead high. The ears are short and broad with a loose flap hanging down at the corner of the mouth and a prominent rounded lobe partially covering the ear aperture. The tail is enclosed in the tail-membrane.

Size. Head-body: 65-75 mm. Tail: 40-50 mm. Forearm: 40-50 mm. **Weight.** 10-18 g. Females are larger than males.

Behaviour. Active at night and after sunset, they roost by day in tree hollows, under loose bark, in rock crevices and buildings, clumping together in colonies of up to 100 bats. The males and most of the juvenile females disperse after the breeding season. They have long narrow wings and fly fast and direct in the upper layers of the forest canopy and in open areas hunting for insects. In cold climates when food is scarce they become torpid. In Tasmania they hibernate from late autumn to early spring. They have good sight and use echo-location to navigate and detect insects, making an audible high-pitched sound in flight. Other vocalisations include buzzes, squeaks and chirps.

Development. Females breed in their first year. In the south they mate in May. Females store the sperm until fertilisation in July, and give birth in November or December. Northern bats give birth in September or October. Twins are usually born and attach to teats in the mother's armpit. They are carried by the mother until well-furred and then left at the roost. They are independent at 2-3 months and live to 5 years or more.

Food. Insects.

Habitat. Closed and open forests, mallee, tall shrublands and urban areas.

Status. Common. Subspecies: *C. g. gouldii* in the south; *C. g. venatoris* in the north.

Nyctophilus arnhemensis

Chalinolobus gouldii

Chalinolobus morio CHOCOLATE WATTLED BAT

A winged placental mammal, the Chocolate Wattled Bat has soft dense fur a uniform chocolate brown above and below. The muzzle is short and the forehead high with a ridge of fur between the eyes and snout. The ears are relatively small and rounded with a small lobe at the bottom of the ear and at the corner of the bottom lip. The eyes are small and the tail protrudes slightly beyond the edge of the tail-membrane.

Size. Head-body: 50-60 mm. Tail: 40-50 mm. Forearm: 35-43 mm. **Weight.** 7-14 g. Females are larger than males.

Behaviour. Active at night and soon after sunset, they roost by day in tree hollows, abandoned bird nests, rock crevices, buildings and caves, alone or in colonies of up to several hundred bats, staying within a home range of about 5 km. They have long narrow wings, fly fast between the tree canopy and understorey, sweeping low over forest trails hunting for insects. They are manoeuvrable in flight, making agile attacking movements and taking off from the ground if necessary. They hibernate in cold climates when food is short, entering hibernation later and emerging earlier than other bats in the same habitat to take advantage of food resources. They have good sight and use echo-location to navigate and detect insects.

Development. Males produce sperm in spring and store it until mating in autumn. The female stores this sperm until fertilisation in early spring. Females give birth to 1-2 young in late spring or early summer (depending on the latitude and climate). Newborn suckle from teats in the mother's armpits, are carried until well-furred and become independent in January or February.

Food. Insects.

Habitat. Wet and dry sclerophyll forests, woodlands and arid regions.

Status. Common.

Chalinolobus nigrogriseus HOARY BAT

Previously confused with *C. picatus* (an inhabitant of the dry inland regions of eastern Australia) the Hoary Bat lacks the white strip of fur along the flanks of the former. This species has grey-black fur, frosted with white hairs in the northern subspecies. Eastern bats are darker. The forehead is high and the head foreshortened. The ears are relatively short and rounded with a small horizontal lobe extending from the bottom of the ear. The eyes are small and the tail is enclosed in the tail-membrane.

Size. Head-body: 45-55 mm. Tail: 35-45 mm. Forearm: 30-40 mm. **Weight.** 7-10 g.

Behaviour. Active mainly at night, they roost by day in tree hollows and rock crevices. One of the first bats to emerge after sunset, they fly moderately fast and direct, hunting close to the ground in clearings, over small water bodies or above the tree canopy, taking insects from the foliage, on the ground or in flight. They are very manoeuvrable, responding to targets 3-5 m away, deviating to catch evasive insects on the wing. They have good sight and use echo-location to navigate and detect insects.

Development. Little is known about their development. Females give birth to 1-2 young in November. Newborn suckle from teats in the mother's armpits, and are weaned in January.

Food. Insects.

Habitat. Wet sclerophyll forests, rainforests, woodlands, heath, and scrub areas around sand dunes.

Status. Common. Subspecies: *C. n. nigrogriseus* eastern Australia and New Guinea; *C. n. rogersi* northern Australia to the west of Cape York.

Chalinolobus morio

Chalinolobus nigrogriseus

Scotorepens sanborni
LITTLE NORTHERN BROAD-NOSED BAT

Emerging just after sundown, this winged placental mammal has long soft fur, brown tinged with red above and paler below. The head is broad with a squarish outline if viewed from above. The muzzle is sparsely-haired with glandular swellings. The forehead is low. The eyes small and the ears broadly rounded with a narrow pointed lobe partially covering the aperture. The tail is enclosed in the tail-membrane. This species has only two upper incisor teeth.
Size. Head-body: 48-52 mm. Tail: 31-34 mm. Forearm: 31-35 mm.
Weight. 6-8 g. Females are usually larger than males.
Behaviour. Active at night and soon after sunset, they roost by day in tree hollows and abandoned buildings, forming small colonies and probably dispersing in winter. They are aggressive if handled. Flight is fast and manoeuvrable with much diving and darting to catch insects detected in the forest understorey, above watercourses, calm coastal bays and street lights. They have good sight and use echo-location to navigate and detect their prey.
Development. Little is known about their development. They probably mate in May or June and give birth to a single young in October or November which suckles from a teat in the mother's armpit.
Food. Flying insects.
Habitat. Rainforests and woodlands.
Status. Common.

Chalinolobus dwyeri
LARGE PIED BAT

Distinguished from the similar Little Pied Bat (*C. picatus*) by its larger ears and longer forearm, this insectivorous winged placental mammal has velvety glossy black fur. A white strip on the underside adjacent to the wing and tail membranes forms a V-shape in the pubic region. The forehead is high and the muzzle short with glandular swellings. The ears have a horizontal lobe at the bottom that extends towards the corner of the mouth. A broad rounded lobe covers the base of the ear aperture. The tail is enclosed in the tail-membrane.
Size. Head-body: 45-55 mm. Tail: 40-46 mm. Forearm: 38-42 mm. **Weight**. 7-10 g.
Behaviour. Active at night and after sunset, they roost by day in caves, mine tunnels and the abandoned, bottle-shaped mud nests of Fairy Martins, forming mixed colonies during the breeding season. Females form nursery colonies in late spring and disperse during the autumn. They have short broad wings, fly moderately fast with high manoeuvrability and hunt for small flying insects below the forest canopy. In the southern part of their range they probably hibernate during the coldest months when food is scarce. They have good sight and use echo-location to navigate and detect insects.
Development. Females become sexually mature at about 12 months and give birth to 1-2 young in late November or December. Newborn suckle from teats in the mother's armpits.
Food. Insects.
Habitat. Dry sclerophyll forests and woodlands.
Status. Sparse.

Scotorepens sanborni

Chalinolobus dwyeri

Scoteanax rueppellii

GREATER BROAD-NOSED BAT

Emerging just after sundown, this winged placental mammal can be identified by its broad head which has a squarish outline from above, and the sparsely-haired muzzle with glandular swellings. The fur is long and soft, dark reddish-brown to dark brown above, and slightly paler below. The forehead is low, the eyes small and the ears broadly rounded with a narrow pointed lobe partially covering the aperture. The tail is enclosed in the tail-membrane. This species has only two upper incisor teeth, distinguishing it from the externally similar Great Pipistrelle (*Falsistrellus tasmaniensis*) which occurs in the same area and has four upper incisors.

Size. Head-body: 80-95 mm. Tail: 40-55 mm. Forearm: 50-56 mm. **Weight.** 23-35 g.
Behaviour. Active at night and after sunset, they roost by day in tree hollows and abandoned buildings, and are aggressive to other bats. They fly slowly with poor manoeuvrability between the canopy and understorey of forests, in paddocks and above water, hunting flying insects, other small bats and mice. They have good sight and use echo-location to navigate and detect their prey.
Development. Little is known about their development. A single young is born in January and suckles from a teat in the mother's armpit.
Food. Insects, bats, mice and other small vertebrates.
Habitat. Wet sclerophyll forests, rainforests and moist gullies.
Status. Sparse to rare.

Myotis adversus

LARGE-FOOTED MYOTIS

A small coastal bat, the Large-footed Myotis is a winged placental mammal with grey-brown to dark brown fur above, slightly paler below and frosted with silver-grey on the chest. Older bats become ginger. Albinism and partial albinism are frequently seen. The ears are large and funnel-shaped with a long pointed lobe partially covering the aperture. The feet are large with a very long ankle bone. The tail is enclosed in the tail-membrane.

Size. Head-body: 52-56 mm. Tail: 36-42 mm.
Forearm: 36-41 mm. **Weight.** 7-12 g.
Behaviour. Active mainly at night, they roost during the day in caves, tunnels, buildings, among dense foliage and dead pandanus leaves, always in the vicinity of fresh water. They congregate in colonies of 10 to several hundred. Males establish and defend a territory shared with a harem of several females during the breeding season. They often hunt in pairs near the banks of water bodies, flying fast, usually less than 400 mm above the surface, catching flying insects or raking the surface of the water with their large feet for aquatic insects and small fish. They have good sight and use echo-location to navigate and detect insects.
Development. Females give birth to a single young in November or December in the southeast. In southern Qld they give birth in early October and again in late January. In the north they breed throughout the year, producing three litters. Newborn suckle from teats in the mother's armpits, remaining with her for some 4 weeks after weaning until they are able to catch their own food.
Food. Insects and small fish.
Habitat. Wet sclerophyll forests and rainforests near creeks and lakes.
Status. Locally common to rare. Subspecies: *M. a. macropus* eastern Australia; *M. a. moluccarum* northern Australia. Also in the western Pacific, eastern Indonesia and Melanesia.

Scoteanax rueppellii

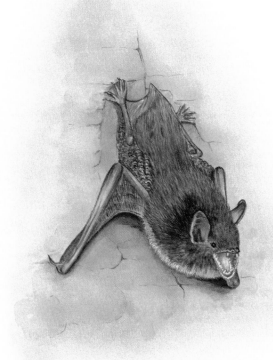

Myotis adversus

Scotorepens greyii

LITTLE BROAD-NOSED BAT

Widely distributed in mainland Australia, this aggressive winged
placental mammal has long soft fur, chestnut-brown, grey-
brown, sandy-brown or ginger above and often lighter below.
The head is broad with a low forehead and squarish outline
if viewed from above. The sparsely-haired muzzle has
glandular swellings and slightly protruding nostrils.
The eyes are small and the ears broadly rounded with a
rounded lobe partially covering the aperture. The tail
protrudes slightly from the tail-membrane. This species
has only two upper incisor teeth, distinguishing it from the
externally similar *Eptesicus baverstocki* which occurs in the same
area and has four upper incisors, the first two being forked.
Size. Head-body: 45-55 mm. Tail: 25-40 mm. Forearm: 28-34 mm. **Weight.** 4-12 g.
Females are usually larger than males.
Behaviour. Active at night and soon after sunset, they roost by day in tree hollows,
hollow fence posts and abandoned buildings with up to 20 other bats. They fly
quickly with darting movements, feeding mainly over waterholes and creeks, and
are able to drink while flying over the surface of still water. They have good sight
and use echo-location to navigate and detect their prey.
Development. Little is known about their development. Mating may occur in April
in southern districts. Females give birth in December, usually to twins. Mating
occurs later in the tropics. Newborn suckle from teats in the mother's armpits.
Food. Flying insects.
Habitat. Wet and dry sclerophyll forests and woodlands, arid areas, sand dunes and
plains.
Status. Common.

Scotorepens balstoni

INLAND BROAD-NOSED BAT

Found in arid inland areas, this aggressive winged placental
mammal is variably coloured from grey to grey-brown, light
brown or dark brown above and lighter below. The head
is broad with a low forehead and squarish outline if
viewed from above. The wide, sparsely-haired muzzle
has glandular swellings and slightly protruding nostrils.
The bottom lip has a V-shaped cleft. The eyes are small
and the ears broadly rounded with a short rounded lobe
partially covering the aperture. The tail is enclosed
in the tail-membrane and is arched under the body at rest and in
flight. This species has only two upper incisor teeth.
Size. Head-body: 50-65 mm. Tail: 25-37 mm. Forearm: 30-38 mm. **Weight.** 7-14 g.
Females are usually larger than males.
Behaviour. Active at night and soon after sunset, they roost by day in tree hollows
and crevices and abandoned buildings, in small colonies, often sharing roosts with
larger colonies of the Little Mastiff-bat (*Mormopterus planiceps*). Fast agile fliers,
they skim over water hunting small flying insects. They have good sight and use
echo-location to navigate and detect their prey.
Development. Mating takes place in late April and early May. Females give birth to
1-3 young (usually twins) in November. Newborn suckle from teats in the mother's
armpits, clinging to her for the first 10 days until they are too heavy to be carried.
They are then left in the roost while she forages, and are weaned at 5 weeks.
Food. Mosquitoes and other flying insects.
Habitat. Arid woodlands and mallee near permanent water.
Status. Common.

Scotorepens greyii

Scotorepens balstoni

Falsistrellus tasmaniensis   TASMANIAN PIPISTRELLE

The largest Tasmanian bat, this winged placental mammal has long soft fur, rich brown to reddish-brown above and slightly paler below. The head has a short, sparsely-haired muzzle with glandular swellings on the sides. The ears are long and narrow with rounded tips, a notch on the outer margin and a narrow, sharply-pointed lobe partially covering the aperture. The tail protrudes slightly from the tail-membrane.

Size. Head-body: 55-70 mm. Tail: 40-50 mm. Forearm: 45-55 mm. **Weight.** 14-26 g.

Behaviour. Active mainly at night, they roost by day in tree hollows, caves and abandoned buildings, often in urban environments, probably forming maternity colonies. They migrate from cold inland sites to warmer coastal areas in winter, hibernating from late autumn to early spring in Tasmania. Their long narrow wings give them limited manoeuvrability and fast direct flight. They have good sight, hunt above or in the upper layers of the forest canopy and use echo-location to navigate and detect their prey.

Development. Males produce sperm in the late summer or autumn when food supplies are plentiful. They store it through the colder months and mate in spring. A single young is born and suckles from a teat in the mother's armpit.

Food. Insects.

Habitat. Wet and dry sclerophyll forests, preferring highland areas.

Status. Sparse.

Pipistrellus westralis   LITTLE PIPISTRELLE

A tiny bat with a delicate body, the Little Pipistrelle is sometimes seen in urban areas in northern Australia catching flying insects around street lamps. A winged placental mammal it is dark brown to black above and lighter below. This bat is very similar to the larger *P. adamsi* of northeastern Qld, and can be distinguished from *Eptesicus* species by the narrow ankle spur that extends along the edge of the tail-membrane. The head has a flattened crown and a sparsely-haired muzzle with glandular swellings on the sides. The ears are broadly triangular with rounded tips and have a triangular lobe partially covering the aperture. The upper jaw has two incisor teeth almost equal in length with slight indentations. The tail is enclosed in the tail-membrane.

Size. Head-body: 34-43 mm. Tail: 29-37 mm. Forearm: 27-31 mm. **Weight.** 3.5-6.5 g.

Behaviour. Active mainly at night, they roost by day in tree hollows and crevices, among dead palm fronds, below the leaf bases of pandans, in mines, caves and under house roofs. They land upright and turn over to hang by their feet or cling to vertical surfaces. Their flight is fast and erratic. They hunt below the forest canopy above the understorey. They have good sight and use echo-location to navigate and detect their prey.

Development. Little is known about their development. They probably breed all year. Females give birth to a single young that suckles from a teat in the mother's armpit.

Food. Flying insects.

Habitat. Rainforests, riverine monsoon forests, paperbark swamps, mangroves and urban areas in coastal and near-coastal sites.

Status. Common.

Falsistrellus tasmaniensis

Pipistrellus westralis

Eptesicus darlingtoni

A small, winged placental mammal, the Large Forest Eptesicus has dark brown to rusty-red fur, becoming very dark brown to black in older bats. The fur has a brown base with light brown or grey tips. The ears and wings are dark brown to black. The forehead rises abruptly from the short muzzle and is well-furred. The ears are rounded with a narrow lobe partially covering the aperture. The tail is enclosed in the tail-membrane.

Size. Head-body: 38-49 mm. Tail: 29-38 mm. Forearm: 31-37 mm.
Weight. 5-8 g. Females are larger than males.
Behaviour. Active mainly at night, they roost by day in tree hollows, crevices and abandoned buildings, alone or in colonies of up to 60 bats. In colder climates they hibernate from late autumn to early spring and emerge to feed on warm days when insects are abroad. They hunt below the forest canopy and around the top of the understorey for flying insects. Their flight is fast with rapid changes of direction. They have good sight and use echo-location to navigate and detect their prey.
Development. Males produce sperm in spring and summer and store it until they mate in autumn. Females store sperm over winter, fertilise their ova in early spring and give birth to a single young in November or December. Newborn suckle from a teat in the mother's armpit and are carried by her until too heavy. They are then left at the roost, and weaned at the end of January or early February.
Food. Insects.
Habitat. Sclerophyll forests and woodlands, often near lakes.
Status. Common.

Eptesicus vulturnus

A small, winged placental mammal, the Small Forest Eptesicus has a dark to mid-grey back, sometimes tinged with brown and a grey belly sometimes flecked with white. The skin on the upper forearms is lighter grey than on the wing membranes. The head is foreshortened with a high forehead and a small furred muzzle. The ears are rounded with a narrow translucent white lobe partially covering the aperture. The tail is enclosed in the tail-membrane.

Size. Head-body: 35-48 mm. Tail: 27-34 mm. Forearm: 25-31 mm.
Weight. 3-6 g. Females are larger than males.
Behaviour. Active mainly at night, they roost by day in tree hollows, timber piles and abandoned buildings, alone or in colonies of up to 50, hanging from the walls or the backs of other bats. Both sexes roost together in winter and hibernate in cold conditions. Females form separate maternity colonies in early summer. They mate with visiting males soon after giving birth and disperse to winter roosts in late autumn. They hunt below the forest canopy and around the top of the understorey, eating larger insects at a perch. Their flight is fast and fluttering with rapid changes of direction. They have good sight and use echo-location to navigate and detect their prey.
Development. Males produce sperm in spring and summer and store it until they mate. Females store the sperm over winter to fertilise their ova in early spring, and give birth to a single young in November or December. Newborn suckle from a teat in the mother's armpit and are carried by her until too heavy. They are then left at the roost and weaned at about 9 weeks.
Food. Insects.
Habitat. Sclerophyll forests and woodlands.
Status. Common.

Eptesicus darlingtoni

Eptesicus vulturnus

Hydromys chrysogaster

WATER-RAT

A rabbit-size placental mammal, the Water-rat is the largest Australian rodent. It has soft, dense, water-repellent fur varying from dark grey to black or brown above, and white, cream or golden yellow below, with a white-tipped tail. The body is streamlined for swimming with a flattened head, long blunt muzzle, small eyes and ears and thick tail used as a rudder. The hindfeet are large and broad with webbing between the toes. They have one pair of upper and lower gnawing incisor teeth, and unlike other rodents have only two molars on each side of the lower jaw.
Size. Head-body: 230-390 mm. Tail: 225-325 mm. **Weight:** 0.34-1.28 kg.
Behaviour. Active mainly at night, they also forage in the early morning and evening, sleeping in a burrow in the bank of a creek with the entrance hidden under roots, or in a hollow log. Burrows run parallel to the bank, and have one or more inner nest chambers some 200 mm high. They are territorial, fighting to establish male and female dominance hierarchies. Sluggish on land, they follow tracks along the water's edge to feeding sites, and swim mostly submerged, diving for food and emerging some distance away, eating their catch on a favourite feeding platform.
Development. Sexually mature at about 12 months, they continue to grow throughout their life of 3-4 years. Breeding occurs throughout the year with peaks in spring and summer. They rear 2-3 litters annually of usually 3-5 young, born some 35 days after mating. Females have four teats and suckle their young for about four weeks. They are independent at about eight weeks.
Food. Fish, crustaceans, molluscs, frogs, water birds, bats and aquatic insects.
Habitat. Close to waterways in most habitats including beaches and urban rivers.
Status. Common to sparse. Also in New Guinea.

Uromys caudimaculatus

WHITE-TAILED RAT

A rabbit-size placental mammal, the Water-rat is one of Australia's largest rodents. It has coarse fur with long spiny guard hairs, grey-brown above and creamy-white below with pale paws. The tail is almost naked with non-overlapping scales; the terminal third is white, the remainder is dark grey mottled with white patches. The muzzle is long with many black whiskers. The eyes and ears are small. The limbs are short with large, strongly-clawed hindfeet. They have one pair of upper and lower gnawing incisor teeth and three pairs of molars on each side of the jaw.
Size. Head-body: 255-365 mm. Tail: 240-360 mm. **Weight:** 245-815 g.
Behaviour. Active mainly at night, they sleep by day in tree hollows, caves and possibly burrows, lined with vegetation. They are found alone or in pairs, and have large home ranges. Males are very aggressive to other males during the breeding season and emit harsh threatening growls. Fast agile climbers, they forage in the forest canopy, using the semi-prehensile tail to grasp branches, bounding up trees, gripping with the forefeet.
Development. Sexually mature at about 10 months, they mate in October or November. Females have four teats and rear 1-3 young born 36-41 days after mating. Newborn cling to the teats and are carried by the mother if she leaves the nest until about 21 days old. They suckle for about 5 weeks and are independent at about 8 weeks.
Food. Nuts (including coconuts), fruits, insects, fungi, small reptiles and eggs. They will enter houses searching for food.
Habitat. Wet sclerophyll forests, rainforests, woodlands.
Status. Common.

Hydromys chrysogaster

Uromys caudimaculatus

Mesembriomys macrurus GOLDEN-BACKED TREE-RAT

A rabbit-size placental mammal, the Golden-backed Tree-rat is an attractive, little-studied rodent of tropical northern Australia. The coarse fur is golden-brown on the back, grading to grey on the sides, and white below. The base of the long tail is grey, the rest white with a brushy tip and overlapping scales. The ears are long and rounded, the eyes bulging and the hindfeet broad with strong claws and well-developed sole pads. They have one pair of upper and lower gnawing incisor teeth and three pairs of molars on each side of the jaw.

Size. Head-body: 180-275 mm. Tail: 290-360 mm. **Weight:** 207-330 g.

Behaviour. Active mainly at night, they sleep by day in tree hollows and among dense foliage in nests of loosely woven leaves. They forage on the ground, on beaches and in trees.

Development. Little is known about their development. Females have four teats and rear 1-2 young.

Food. Foliage, insects and shellfish. They will enter buildings searching for food.

Habitat. High rainfall areas in rugged country with open forests and woodlands with a grassy or shrubby understorey, mangroves, palm forests, pandanus clumps and vine thickets.

Status. Relatively common in remote coastal northwestern Kimberley region of W.A., sparse or rare elsewhere.

Mesembriomys gouldii BLACK-FOOTED TREE-RAT

A rabbit-size placental mammal, this squirrel-like species is one of Australia's largest rodents. The fur is long, coarse and shaggy, grey-brown flecked with black above and creamy-white below. The tail is black with a white brushy tip and overlapping scales. The ears are long and rounded, the eyes bulging and the hindfeet broad with strong claws and well-developed sole pads..They have one pair of upper and lower gnawing incisor teeth and three pairs of molars on each side of the jaw.

Size. Head-body: 250-315 mm. Tail: 310-415 mm. **Weight:** 525-900 g.

Behaviour. Active only at night, they sleep by day in tree hollows, crevices and buildings. Solitary and aggressive, they probably defend their nest site, uttering threatening grumbling and growling sounds before fighting. They are fast runners and agile climbers, often feeding on the ground on fallen fruits, and rapidly ascending a tree if disturbed.

Development. They breed throughout the year with a peak in winter and few births in the wetter months. Females have four teats and usually rear 2 young born 43-44 days after mating. Newborn develop rapidly, clinging to the teats and being carried by the mother if she leaves the nest until fully furred with the eyes open at 10-11 days old. They are weaned at about 28 days.

Food. Nuts, fruits (including pandanus fruits), flowers, insects and snails.

Habitat. Open forests and woodlands with a grassy or shrubby understorey.

Status. Common in N.T., rare in Qld.

Mesembriomys macrurus

Mesembriomys gouldii

Mastacomys fuscus

BROAD-TOOTHED RAT

A stout, thickly-furred placental mammal of the cool highlands, this species derives its name from its unusually broad teeth, enabling it to feed on tough plant material. The long fur is light to dark brown grading to grey below. The tail is short with small bristles and overlapping scales. The head is wide with rounded ears, and the hindfeet are relatively long and slender. They have one pair of upper and lower gnawing incisor teeth and three pairs of molars on each side of the jaw.

Size. Head-body: 140-195 mm. Tail: 100-135 mm. **Weight:** 100-200 g.

Behaviour. Although mainly nocturnal, they are frequently active during the day, sleeping in well-insulated nests of finely-shredded grass under logs or dense vegetation, often button grass. They have overlapping home ranges and move about along tunnels constructed in the undergrowth. Covered in a blanket of snow in winter, these remain warm and dry, allowing them to forage even on the coldest days. Breeding pairs may share nests except when the young are suckling when females become very aggressive to males.

Development. Females are sexually mature at about 12 months, and breed from September to January in Tasmania and from November to February on the mainland. They have four teats and may produce two litters of two young per season born about 35 days after mating. Newborn are well-furred and cling to the mother's teats if disturbed and are dragged behind her. They are weaned at about 30 days.

Food. Stems and leaves of grasses and sedges, bark and seeds.

Habitat. Cool, wet alpine and sub-alpine heathland, woodlands and tall open forests to 2,200 m.

Status. Common to sparse.

Rattus lutreolus

SWAMP RAT

A solidly built, robust placental mammal, the Swamp Rat has long, soft fur, dark grey to grey-brown above and lighter grey or buff below. The tail is short, sparsely-haired with overlapping scales. The ears are short and largely concealed by the fur. The feet are dark grey-brown and the hindfeet are relatively short. Like other rodents they have one pair of upper and lower gnawing incisor teeth and three pairs of molars on each side of the jaw.

Size. Head-body: 120-200 mm. Tail: 80-150 mm. **Weight:** 55-170 g.

Behaviour. Although mainly nocturnal, they are frequently active during the day, sleeping in nests of shredded vegetation in tussock grass, burrow systems, rotting logs or hollows in tree bases. Solitary, in winter they occupy territories of at least 0.2 ha (depending on the availability of food). In the mating season females expand and defend their territories against other females, while males roam through female territories searching for mates. They construct tunnels through dense vegetation to facilitate access to food sources and avoid predators. They can climb and swim fast in emergencies.

Development. Females are sexually mature at about 10 weeks, breed mostly in spring and summer, and produce several litters of 3-4 young in a good season. They have ten teats on the mainland and eight in Tasmania. Young are born 22-23 days after mating, are weaned at 3-4 weeks, and live to about 18 months.

Food. Rhizomes, stems and leaves of sedges and grasses supplemented by insects, mosses and fungi.

Habitat. Coastal swamps, heathland, sclerophyll forests, rainforests and sedgelands.

Status. Common. Subspecies: *R. l. lutreolus* southeastern Australia; *R. l. lacus* Qld; *R. l. velutinus* Tasmania.

Mastacomys fuscus

Rattus lutreolus

Rattus colletti

A placental mammal of the tropical floodplains of northern Australia, the Dusky Rat has long, coarse and spiny fur, grizzled dark brown to black above, yellowish on the sides and throat, and greyish-buff below. The small ears and long, stout, hairy tail are dark brown. Like other rodents they have one pair of upper and lower gnawing incisor teeth and three pairs of molars on each side of the jaw.

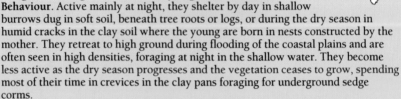

Size. Head-body: 145-210 mm. Tail: 105-150 mm.
Weight: 85-215 g. Males are usually larger than females.
Behaviour. Active mainly at night, they shelter by day in shallow burrows dug in soft soil, beneath tree roots or logs, or during the dry season in humid cracks in the clay soil where the young are born in nests constructed by the mother. They retreat to high ground during flooding of the coastal plains and are often seen in high densities, foraging at night in the shallow water. They become less active as the dry season progresses and the vegetation ceases to grow, spending most of their time in crevices in the clay pans foraging for underground sedge corms.
Development. Females are sexually mature at about 5 weeks. Breeding begins at the end of the wet season and extends to the middle of the dry season. Females have 12 teats and give birth to usually 7-9 young born 21-23 days after mating, and weaned at about 20 days. In good conditions they can produce about 100 young in 6 months.
Food. Grass roots and sedge corms.
Habitat. Coastal floodplains, swamps and tidal rivers fringed with mangroves.
Status. Usually common with dramatic population fluctuations.

Rattus tunneyi

Usually found in tall grasslands, the Pale Field-rat is an attractive rodent with light shiny yellow-brown fur above and grey or cream fur below. The head is broad and rounded with protruding eyes and short rounded ears. The tail is relatively short and sparsely-haired with overlapping scales. Like other rodents they have one pair of upper and lower gnawing incisor teeth and three pairs of molars on each side of the jaw.
Size. Head-body: 120-195 mm. Tail: 80-150 mm.
Weight: 40-165 g.
Behaviour. Active mainly at night, they shelter by day alone or with their offspring in shallow burrow systems dug in loose soil with vertical shafts and horizontal tunnels, often with several entrances marked by large spoil heaps. They appear to live in patchy colonies, using well-marked runways through the thick grass between their burrows. Docile, curious and easily handled, they will enter houses searching for food.
Development. Females are sexually mature at about 5 weeks. Breeding extends from March to May on the east coast, and May to August in the north and west. Females have 10 teats and may rear several litters of usually 4-5 young in quick succession. Pregnancy lasts 21-22 days. Young are furred at 7 days, have their eyes open at 18 days, and are weaned at 21 days.
Food. Grass roots, stems and seeds.
Habitat. Tall grasslands, mangroves, sand dunes, open forests with a grassy understorey, canefields and Hoop Pine plantations.
Status. Common. Subspecies: *R. t. tunneyi* north and northwestern Australia; *R. t. culmorum* eastern Australia.

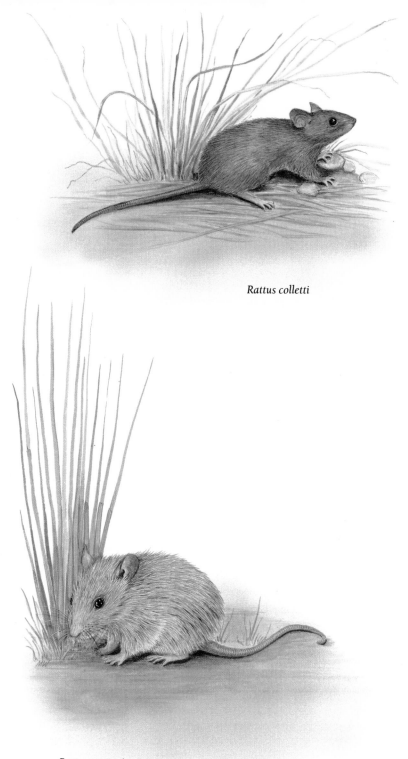

Rattus colletti

Rattus tunneyi

Rattus fuscipes

Abundant in the dense forest understorey, this placental mammal has dense soft fur, grey to grey-brown or slightly reddish above and grey or cream below. The tail is grey to brown, sparsely-haired with overlapping scales. The soles of the hindfeet are pale, distinguishing it from the Swamp Rat (*R. lutreolus*) which has black soles. They have one pair of upper and lower gnawing incisor teeth and three pairs of molars on each side of the jaw.

Size. Head-body: 110-205 mm. Tail: 105-195 mm. **Weight:** 65-225 g.

Behaviour. Active mainly at night, they shelter by day in short burrows often under logs or stones with a sloping, twisting tunnel leading to a vegetation-lined nest chamber some 150 mm diameter and 350-450 mm below ground. Adults live alone or with their young, occupying a home range of some 200 m diameter, often overlapping with other rats. The young leave early and establish a small home range with access to sufficient resources to survive the winter. Males extend their home ranges in spring and roam over large areas.

Development. Females are sexually mature at about 3 months. They breed throughout the year with peaks of births in late spring and summer. Females have 10 teats (sometimes 8 in the northern subspecies) and give birth to usually 5 young born 22-25 days after mating. Their eyes are open by 3 weeks and they are weaned at about 4 weeks. Most adults die during their first winter in cooler climates, although they may live to 2 years.

Food. Insects, supplemented by fungi and other vegetation.

Habitat. Rainforests and sclerophyll forests with dense ground cover.

Status. Common. Subspecies: *R. f. fuscipes* W.A.; *R. f. greyi* S.A. and western Vic.; *R. f. assimilis* east coast; *R. f. coracius* Cape York.

Rattus villosissimus

Also known as the Plague Rat, this desert species undergoes dramatic population increases after several wet years. The fur is long and grey above with conspicuous black guard hairs and light grey below. The tail is grey to black with prominent dark hairs and overlapping scales. Like other rodents they have one pair of upper and lower gnawing incisor teeth and three pairs of molars on each side of the jaw.

Size. Head-body: 140-225 mm. Tail: 120-190 mm. **Weight:** 105-290 g.

Behaviour. Active mainly at night, they shelter by day in short burrows 200-300 mm deep with several entrances, grouped in grassy depressions near trees, bushes or rocks with spoil heaps at the entrances and several well-worn runways between them. Females build spherical nests of shredded vegetation in a central chamber 100-150 mm diameter. Adults live alone or with their young, and may utilise several burrows. In plague years they wander in vast numbers over the countryside, invading camps and homesteads in their thousands.

Development. Females are sexually mature at about 10 weeks. They breed throughout the year with lulls from mid-winter to early spring. Females have 12 teats and give birth to usually 6-7 young born 21-23 days after mating. Their eyes are open at 17 days and they are weaned at about 3 weeks.

Food. Grasses, herbs, seeds and insects. During plagues they become cannibalistic and will attempt to eat any organic material. They need water and retreat to moist areas during droughts.

Habitat. Most habitats in arid to semi-arid areas with access to drinking water.

Status. Usually rare and scattered, with huge population increases after several years of high rainfall.

Rattus fuscipes

Rattus villosissimus

Rattus leucopus

CAPE YORK RAT

Also found in the rainforests of Cape York and New Guinea, this placental mammal has coarse and spiny fur, blackish-brown to golden-brown or reddish above and white or grey below. The head is pointed with large ears sparsely covered with buff to reddish-brown hairs. The tail is slender and tapering, almost hairless, often mottled brown or grey, with off-white patches in far northern Australia. The pale hindfeet are stout and long. Like other rodents they have one pair of upper and lower gnawing incisor teeth and three pairs of molars on each side of the jaw.

Size. Head-body: 130-210 mm. Tail: 135-200 mm. **Weight:** 70-215 g.

Behaviour. Active mainly at night, they shelter by day in cracks and crevices or under boulders and logs. No burrows or runways have been detected. Shy, unobtrusive and little-studied, they are sparsely distributed and probably solitary.

Development. Females are sexually mature at about 3 months. They breed throughout the year with a lull from June to early September. Females have 6 teats and give birth to usually 2-5 young born 22-24 days after mating. Their eyes are open by 22 days and they are weaned at about 25 days.

Food. Insects, supplemented by fungi, herbs, seeds and fruit.

Habitat. Tropical rainforests.

Status. Common. Subspecies: *R. l. leucopus* northern Cape York Peninsula; *R. l. cooktownensis* southern Cape York Peninsula. Extends to New Guinea.

Rattus sordidus

CANEFIELD RAT

Sugar cane growers have created an ideal habitat for this species of the tropical grasslands and open forests, and now regard it as a serious pest. A short-limbed placental mammal, the Canefield Rat has coarse and spiny fur grizzled dark brown to black above with prominent guard hairs, and light grey or buff below. The tail is dark brown to black with prominent overlapping scales. The soles of the hindfeet are pale, distinguishing it from the similar Swamp Rat (*R. lutreolus*) which has dark soles. Like other rodents they have one pair of upper and lower gnawing incisor teeth and three pairs of molars on each side of the jaw.

Size. Head-body: 120-210 mm. Tail: 100-160 mm. **Weight:** 50-260 g.

Behaviour. Although predominantly nocturnal, large populations are active during the day. They rest in extensive burrow systems about 400 mm deep with tunnels 50-100 mm diameter sloping down to a nest chamber about 150 mm diameter lined with dry grass. The entrances are near grass clumps, stones and stumps. Burrows are often concentrated in dense colonies with networks of runways between them. As many as 23 non-breeding adults have been found in one nest chamber, although females with young force other adults out.

Development. Females are sexually mature at 9-10 weeks. They breed at any time of year with the majority of births from March to May. Females have 12 teats and usually give birth to 6 young 20-27 days after mating. Young are fully furred at 7 days, have their eyes open at 18 days and are weaned at 3 weeks. They have the highest reproductive potential of all the native true rats, and may reach plague proportions in canefields.

Food. Grass, seeds, leaves, sugar cane stems and insects.

Habitat. Tropical grasslands with dense ground cover, open forests, grassy clearings in rainforests and canefields.

Status. Common in northern areas, rare in the southern part of its range.

Rattus leucopus

Rattus sordidus

Rattus rattus

BLACK RAT

Introduced by the Europeans, the Black Rat is common in coastal Australia. This slender placental mammal has sleek, smooth coat, charcoal grey to black or light brown above and cream or white below. The head is long and pointed with large thin ears over 20 mm long, protruding eyes and long black whiskers. The tail is long and naked with overlapping scales. Like other rodents they have one pair of upper and lower gnawing incisor teeth and three pairs of molars on each side of the jaw. They may carry the plague bacillus and transmit other diseases to humans through their excreta.

Size. Head-body: 165-205 mm. Tail: 185-255 mm. **Weight**: 95-340 g.
Behaviour. Active mainly at night, they shelter in nests of shredded material in roofs, cavity walls, trees, shallow scrapes or extensive shallow burrow systems often around farm buildings or river banks. They are timid when cornered, but will defend a territory (scent-marked by rubbing with the cheek or belly) against intruders. Territorial groups establish a hierarchy with a dominant resident male and subordinates. They can climb and swim well.
Development. Sexually mature at 3-4 months, they live about 1 year in the wild and breed throughout the year, producing up to six litters, giving birth to usually 5-10 young 21-22 days after mating. Females have 10-12 teats. Young are born blind and naked and are weaned at 20 days.
Food. Nuts, eggs, seeds, insects, underground fungi, small mammals and birds.
Habitat. Around watercourses in disturbed areas and human habitations.
Status. Common.

Rattus norvegicus

BROWN RAT

Introduced by the Europeans, the Brown Rat is very common in urban areas and around farm buildings. This thickset placental mammal has shaggy, bristly fur, grey-brown above and white to grey below. The ears are small and rounded, close set and up to 20 mm long. The muzzle is blunt with long whiskers. The tail is stout, paler below, short and naked with overlapping scales. The pink hindfeet have long toes and pale soles. Like other rodents they have one pair of upper and lower gnawing incisor teeth and three pairs of molars on each side of the jaw.

Size. Head-body: 180-255 mm. Tail: 150-215 mm. **Weight**: 200-480 g.
Behaviour. Active mainly at night, they shelter under bushes, in sewers and other sites in urban areas, or construct deep extensive burrow systems, huddling together in nests of shredded material carried in the mouth. Colonies of several hundred are formed. Members are recognised by smell and live within a home range of some 30 m diameter. Dominant males have exclusive territories around burrows containing several breeding females. Young rats are forced to leave the colony. Very exploratory, they will sample all food sources, and move along runways following odour trails. They can climb and swim well, but prefer to live at ground level.
Development. Sexually mature at 6-8 weeks, they breed throughout the year, usually giving birth to 7-10 young 21-23 days after mating. Females have 12 teats. Young are well-furred at 10 days, open their eyes at 15-20 days, and are weaned at 20 days.
Food. Shellfish, eggs, seeds, insects, small mammals and birds. They hoard food in the nest, carrying it in their cheeks, manipulating it with the hands.
Habitat. Cellars, sewers, creek banks, farm buildings and warehouses.
Status. Common.

Rattus rattus

Rattus norvegicus

Melomys cervinipes

FAWN-FOOTED MELOMYS

A rat-size placental mammal, the Fawn-footed Melomys has long, soft, fine fur, sandy-brown to dark grey-brown above and white, cream or grey below. The naked tail is partially prehensile with non-overlapping scales. They have a thick-necked appearance with short rounded ears, a broad head, bulging eyes, long dark whiskers and broad hindfeet. They have one pair of upper and lower gnawing incisor teeth and three pairs of molars on each side of the jaw.

Size. Head-body: 95-200 mm. Tail: 115-210 mm. **Weight:** 45-115 g.
Behaviour. Active mainly at night, they sleep by day in grass-lined nests in trees, shrubs and pandanus fronds, utilising burrows occasionally for refuge. They probably form stable breeding pairs and occupy distinct home ranges of some 70 m diameter. Agile climbers, they forage in and around trees, climbing creepers and vines, using the tail for balance and as a fifth limb, leaping short distances between branches. They can also swim if necessary.
Development. They breed throughout the year with a peak from August to February, producing up to five litters per year. Females have four teats and usually rear two young born about 38 days after mating. Newborn cling to the teats and are carried by the mother if she leaves the nest until fully furred at about 10 days old. They are weaned at about 20 days.
Food. Leaves, shoots, fruits and seeds.
Habitat. Wet sclerophyll forests, rainforests, pandanus clumps, mangroves.
Status. Common. Threatened by rainforest clearing.

Melomys burtoni

GRASSLAND MELOMYS

A rat-size placental mammal, the Grassland Melomys is considered a pest by sugar-cane farmers who have created favourable new habitats for this rodent by clearing the forests. The fur is long and soft, grey-brown to reddish-brown or khaki above, sometimes with pale orange flanks, and white, grey or cream below. The slender tail is partially prehensile, dark brown and naked with small non-overlapping scales. They have a thick-necked appearance with short rounded ears, a broad head, bulging eyes, long whiskers and broad hindfeet. They have one pair of upper and lower gnawing incisor teeth and three pairs of molars on each side of the jaw.

Size. Head-body: 85-140 mm. Tail: 90-150 mm. **Weight:** 25-80 g.
Behaviour. Active at night, they sleep by day in spherical nests 200-500 mm diameter of shredded leaves and grass woven around stout grass stems, above the ground, or in trees. Short burrows are sometimes constructed. They are very aggressive if confined, and occupy distinct home ranges of up to 0.4 ha. Agile climbers, they forage in tall reeds, sedges and sugar-cane using the partly prehensile tail for balance and grip. They can cross waterways by swimming or rafting.
Development. They breed throughout the year with a peak in autumn and winter in the north, and in spring and summer in the south, depending on the rainfall. Females have four teats and usually rear 2-3 young. Newborn develop rapidly, clinging to the teats and being carried by the mother if she leaves the nest until fully furred with the eyes open at 7-10 days old. They are weaned at about 20 days.
Food. Grass stems, seeds, berries, sugar-cane and insects.
Habitat. Grasslands, open forests and woodlands close to water.
Status. Abundant in sugar-cane areas, sparse to rare elsewhere.

Melomys cervinipes

Melomys burtoni

Zyzomys argurus

The size of a large mouse, this compact placental mammal is found in areas where roughly dissected rocks provide nesting sites. The coarse fur is golden brown above and white below. The sparsely-haired tail has overlapping scales, is swollen at the base with fat deposits and is easily lost. The soles of the feet are smooth, the eyes are large and bulging, the ears rounded, and the muzzle protruding with long whiskers. Like other rodents they have one pair of upper and lower gnawing incisor teeth and three pairs of molars on each side of the jaw.

Size. Head-body: 85-140 mm. Tail: 90-125 mm. **Weight:** 29-65 g.

Behaviour. Active at night, they sleep in nests in rock crevices, probably living in close proximity in cool rocky refuges. They are very susceptible to heat stress and soon die if exposed to the hot sun. Little is known about their behaviour. They fight ferociously when first caged together, and may establish dominance hierarchies in the wild. Few are seen towards the end of the wet season when they probably form breeding pairs.

Development. Sexually mature at 5-6 months, they breed at any time with a peak from April to June. Females have four teats and rear 1-4 young born about 35 days after mating. Young are are left in the nest while the mother forages. They are fully-furred at 10 days, have their eyes open eyes at 12 days, are independent at about 4 weeks and live to 2 years.

Food. Plant stems, leaves, seeds, grasses, fungi and insects.

Habitat. Woodlands, low open forests and grasslands, always in rocky areas. They are excluded from wetter closed forest areas by the Large Rock-rat (*Z. woodwardi*). Externally similar although larger and more robust, this rare rodent occupies similar habitats in the N.T. and northeastern W.A.

Status. Common.

Conilurus penicillatus

An attractive placental mammal of tropical northern Australia and New Guinea. This rodent has long coarse fur, light grizzled grey-brown above and creamy-white below. The tail is grey-brown at the base with a black or sometimes white brushy tip and overlapping scales. Solidly built, the Brush-tailed Tree-rat has a rabbit-like appearance with very long ears, large bulging eyes, a broad blunt head and elongated hindfeet. Like other rodents they have one pair of upper and lower gnawing incisor teeth and three pairs of molars on each side of the jaw.

Size. Head-body: 150-200 mm. Tail: 180-215 mm. **Weight:** 110-170 g.

Behaviour. Active at night, they sleep by day in tree hollows, crevices, pandanus leaves and buildings. Little is known about their behaviour. They spend most of their time in trees, climbing up to 15 m above the ground foraging for food, descending occasionally, climbing rapidly if disturbed and uttering a threatening growl if cornered.

Development. They probably breed throughout the year with a peak from May to August, with few births in the wetter months. Females have four teats and usually rear 2 young born 33-36 days after mating. Newborn develop rapidly. They are fully-furred with the eyes open at 10 days and weaned at about 20 days.

Food. Grass, herbs, seeds and fruits.

Habitat. Open eucalypt forests and woodlands, rainforests, pandanus scrub, often on the seashore near large casuarina trees.

Status. Sparse. Also in southern New Guinea.

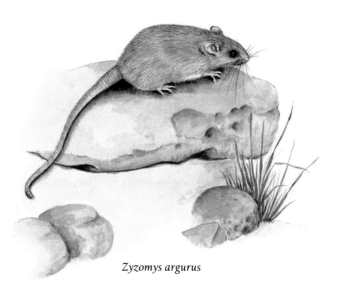

Zyzomys argurus

Conilurus penicillatus

Pseudomys albocinereus

ASH-GREY MOUSE

A small attractive rodent, the Ash-grey Mouse is restricted to semi-arid regions of Western Australia. The long soft fur is silver grey tinged with fawn above and white below. The nose, feet and tail are bright pink, the bulging eyes have prominent dark eyelashes, and the muzzle has long black or white whiskers. The ears are large and rounded, the tail slightly hairy with overlapping scales. Like other rodents they have one pair of upper and lower gnawing incisor teeth and three pairs of molars on each side of the jaw.

Size. Head-body: 63-110 mm. Tail: 85-115 mm. **Weight:** 14-40 g.

Behaviour. Active at night, they sleep by day in cool burrows some 600 mm below ground and up to 4 m long with a small pile of excavated soil at the entrance, sometimes with side tunnels and interconnecting nest chambers. Breeding pairs with their young often occupy the same burrow.

Development. They breed throughout the year with a peak from April to September, depending on the rainfall. Females have four teats and usually rear four young born 37-38 days after mating. They open their eyes at 15 days and are weaned at about 25 days.

Food. Seeds, plant material, lichen and insects. They can probably survive without drinking.

Habitat. Semi-arid tussock grasslands, tall shrublands, open sandplains with heath vegetation and woodlands.

Status. Common. Subspecies: *P. a. albocinereus* on the mainland; *P. a. squalorum* on Bernier Island.

Pseudomys australis

PLAINS RAT

One of Australia's most attractive rodents, the Plains Rat is a desert species with a silver sheen to its soft, thick fur. Sandy-brown to grey above and white to cream below, this placental mammal is quite bulky with large ears, bulging eyes and a well-furred tail, brown or grey above and white below with a lighter tip. Like other rodents they have one pair of upper and lower gnawing incisor teeth and three pairs of molars on each side of the jaw.

Size. Head-body: 100-140 mm. Tail: 80-120 mm.

Weight: 50-80 g.

Behaviour. Active at night, they sleep by day in cool shallow burrows dug into the hard gibber with the entrances concealed below bushes or cattle dung. About 1 m long and up to 300 mm deep, they have a single nest chamber often stuffed with vegetation. They establish dominance hierarchies and form colonies within a defined territory, building their burrows some 10 m apart connected by surface runways. Up to 20 rats may occupy a single burrow out of the breeding season, although when breeding a single male will share with two or three females. Colonies rapidly increase or decrease in size depending on food sources and predators. When alarmed they stand up on their hindlegs and squeal. They have a fairly extensive vocal repertoire of chirps, screeches and whistles.

Development. Females are sexually mature at about 8 weeks. They breed mostly in winter and spring, probably rearing several litters in succession. Females have four teats and usually rear four young born 30-31 days after mating. They open their eyes at 15 days and are weaned at about 30 days.

Food. Green plants, seeds and insects. They can survive without drinking.

Habitat. Arid gibber plains, river flats, sandridges with low shrubs.

Status. Common.

Pseudomys albocinereus

Pseudomys australis

Pseudomys novaehollandiae

NEW HOLLAND MOUSE

Very similar to the introduced House Mouse (*Mus musculus*), but lacking the distinctive odour, this small placental mammal can be distinguished by the tail which is dusky brown above and white below, larger ears and eyes, and a dark stripe sometimes along the centre of the head. The fur is grey-brown often grizzled with long dark hairs above, and grey-white below. The feet are slender and covered with white hairs. Females have four teats, unlike the House Mouse which has five teats. Like other rodents they have one pair of upper and lower gnawing incisor teeth and three pairs of molars on each side of the jaw.

Size. Head-body: 65-95 mm. Tail: 79-110 mm. **Weight:** 10-24 g.

Behaviour. Active mainly at night, they sleep in burrows up to 5 m long with a nest chamber, probably shared by family groups, or shelter in shallow temporary burrows. They utilise separate home ranges, although those of mature females may overlap, with up to 17 animals per hectare in good conditions.

Development. Females are sexually mature at 4 months, and may produce their first litter in the year of birth. The breeding season extends from August to January, with up to four litters per year of 3-4 young born 29-33 days after mating. They open their eyes at 15 days, are weaned at 3-4 weeks and live 18-24 months.

Food. Leaves, seeds, flowers, fungi, moss, roots and insects.

Habitat. Open forests, dry heathland and areas regenerating after fire.

Status. Common.

Pseudomys higginsi

LONG-TAILED RAT

Found only in Tasmania, the Long-tailed Rat has very soft and dense fur forming a prominent ridge between the eyes. Dark grey-brown above fading to fawn on the sides and grey white below, this placental mammal has a very long bicoloured tail, dark grey above and white below, carried curved up well clear of the ground. The ears are large and round, the hindfeet are long and slender and clothed with white hairs. Like other rodents they have one pair of upper and lower gnawing incisor teeth and three pairs of molars on each side of the jaw.

Size. Head-body: 115-150 mm. Tail: 145-200 mm. **Weight:** 50-90 g.

Behaviour. Active mainly at night, they often forage by day in the winter, sleeping in nests of shredded bark or grass in a hole in a rotting stump or log, beneath leaf litter, or at the end of a short burrow. Placid, curious and highly sociable, they remain in a small home range and form permanent breeding pairs, sharing a nest with their offspring and defending a territory. Up to 10 families per hectare can be found in good conditions. They are good climbers, poor swimmers, leap randomly if threatened, and make a faint high-pitched whistle when disturbed.

Development. The breeding season extends from October to March, with two litters per year. Females have four teats and usually give birth to three young born 31-32 days after mating. Newborn are well-furred and cling to the mother's teats if disturbed and are dragged behind her, otherwise being left in the nest with the entrance temporarily plugged while the mother forages. They open their eyes at 15 days, are weaned at 25-30 days and live to about 18 months.

Food. Grass, seeds, fruits, insects and spiders.

Habitat. Wet closed forests with more than 2,000 mm of rain per year.

Status. Common.

Pseudomys novaehollandiae

Pseudomys higginsi

Pseudomys delicatulus

DELICATE MOUSE

A tiny placental mammal, the Delicate Mouse is Australia's smallest native rodent. Dainty and graceful in appearance, this species has yellow-brown to grey-brown fur above and white or cream below. The nose and feet are bright pink, the tail is slender with overlapping scales. The ears are quite large and rounded (10-13 mm long), the eyes large and bulging. Like other rodents they have one pair of upper and lower gnawing incisor teeth and three pairs of molars on each side of the jaw.

Size. Head-body: 55-75 mm. Tail: 55-80 mm. **Weight:** 6-15 g.

Behaviour. Active mainly at night, they sleep by day in grass-lined nests in burrows, hollow logs or under bark. Burrows are short and shallow in hard granite soils with false passages and a single nest chamber. In soft soil they may be up to 400 mm deep with a single tunnel to 2 m long terminating in a grass-lined spherical nest chamber. Spoil heaps to 100 mm high are found by the entrance.

Development. Reaching sexual maturity at 10-11 months, they usually mate in June and July, producing several litters in favourable conditions. Females have four teats and normally give birth to 3-4 young born 28-31 days after mating. Newborn weigh only 1 g and are some 25 mm long. Their eyes open at 20 days, and they are fully-furred and weaned at 30 days.

Food. Seeds of native grasses.

Habitat. Coastal sand dunes with sparse vegetation of grasses, herbs and stunted trees; low woodlands, open scrublands and hummock grasslands.

Status. Sparse to locally common, with marked seasonal population fluctuations.

Subspecies: *P. d. delicatus* on the mainland; *P. d. mimula* on Groote Eylandt.

Pseudomys nanus

WESTERN CHESTNUT MOUSE

A small rodent of the tropical north of Australia, the Western Chestnut Mouse is very similar in appearance to the larger, slightly lighter-coloured Eastern Chestnut Mouse (*P. gracilicaudatus*) of the east coast of NSW and Qld. Light fawn-orange with many long dark brown hairs above, with light orange-brown flanks, a pronounced light eye ring and a white belly, this placental mammal has a naked tail with overlapping scales. The ears are small and round, the limbs short and the body stout. Like other rodents they have one pair of upper and lower gnawing incisor teeth and three pairs of molars on each side of the jaw.

Size. Head-body: 84-140 mm. Tail: 70-140 mm. **Weight:** 25-80 g.

Behaviour. Active mainly at night, they probably sleep by day in grass nests, although they have not been studied in the wild. They fight in captivity and utter frequent high-pitched whistling calls when active.

Development. They breed most of the year except in dry periods during September and November, probably rearing several litters in rapid succession to take advantage of good conditions in a habitat subject to fires and flooding. Females have four teats and usually give birth to three young born 22-24 days after mating. Young are furred at 7 days, have their eyes open at 12 days and are weaned at about 21 days.

Food. Native grasses and seeds. May be able to survive without drinking.

Habitat. Woodlands, tropical tussock grasslands, open forests with good ground cover on rocky or sandy soil.

Status. Common. Subspecies: *P. n. nanus* on the mainland; *P. n. ferculinus* on Barrow Island.

Pseudomys delicatulus

Pseudomys nanus

Pseudomys hermannsburgensis SANDY INLAND MOUSE

A small placental mammal, the Sandy Inland Mouse is a slender,
slightly-built rodent, and is very similar to the introduced
House Mouse (*Mus musculus*), but lacks the distinctive
odour and has larger ears, eyes and tail. The fur is
sandy-brown to grey above, grading to white below. Like
other rodents they have one pair of upper and lower
gnawing incisor teeth and three pairs of molars on each
side of the jaw.
Size. Head-body: 65-85 mm. Tail: 70-90 mm. **Weight**: 8-15 g.
Behaviour. Active mainly at night, they sleep in grass-lined
nests in deep burrows with a single tunnel dug some 500 mm below the
surface to avoid high temperatures. They are gregarious, sharing their burrows with
others. Social tolerance probably depends on their breeding condition. Small
groups of around six breeding adults have been found in burrows, and 22 non-
breeding adults were discovered in another burrow. Pregnant or lactating females
become intolerant of other adults and have been recorded castrating or killing their
mates.
Development. Reaching sexual maturity at about 3 months, they breed after good
rainfall, producing several litters in favourable conditions. Females have four teats
and normally give birth to 3-4 young born 29-34 days after mating. Young are well-
furred with their eyes open at 20 days, and are independent at 30 days.
Food. Seeds, roots and tubers. They can probably survive without drinking.
Habitat. Woodlands, mallee shrublands, tussock grasslands, gibber plains, alluvial
flats.
Status. Common, widespread.

Leggadina forresti FORREST'S MOUSE

Distinguished by its short stumpy tail, plump body and blunt
muzzle with many long whiskers, Forrest's Mouse is a small
placental mammal of the arid regions of Australia. The
fur is coarse and shiny, yellow-brown to grey above with
scattered dark hairs, pure white below and on the feet.
The tail is grey above and white below with overlapping
scales. The pinkish-grey ears are short and rounded, the
eyes large and bulging. Like other rodents they have one
pair of upper and lower gnawing incisor teeth and three
pairs of molars on each side of the jaw.
Size. Head-body: 65-105 mm. Tail: 50-75 mm. **Weight**: 15-25 g.
Behaviour. Active at night, they sleep by day in grass-lined nests in burrows around
150 mm deep to avoid the heat. Burrows are short, some 400 mm long, with several
blind tunnels and a single nest chamber. They are generally solitary, living alone or
with their young. Females with young are intolerant of other adults.
Development. They breed after rainfall, and may rear several litters in favourable
conditions. Females have four teats and normally give birth to 3-4 young. The
young are well-furred by 10 days, have their eyes open at 20 days, and are weaned
at 28 days.
Food. Seeds and green vegetation. They can probably survive without drinking.
Habitat. Arid and semi-arid habitats including grasslands, low shrublands, mulga
woodlands, sand plains and clay pans.
Status. Sparse, widespread.

Pseudomys hermannsburgensis

Leggadina forresti

Mus musculus HOUSE MOUSE

One of the most adaptable placental mammals in the world, the House Mouse probably originated in central Asia and accompanied humans to Australia. The fur is soft and dense, to 7 mm long, brownish-grey above and white to grey or pale yellow below. The ears are large and rounded, the eyes bulging and the tail sparsely-haired with overlapping scales. Like other rodents they have one pair of upper and lower gnawing incisor teeth and three pairs of molars on each side of the jaw. They have a distinctive musty smell, the inner surface of the upper incisors is notched, and females have 10 teats, distinguishing them from the *Pseudomys*.

Size. Head-body: 60-100 mm. Tail: 75-100 mm. **Weight:** 10-25 g.

Behaviour. Active mainly at night, they rest in nests of shredded material placed in secluded places in buildings, reed beds, cracks in the ground, or at the centre of complex shallow burrow systems with several narrow tunnels and entrances. In buildings they live in small groups of related individuals and defend a fixed territory of about 6 m diameter against strangers. Young adults are forced to disperse. Less defined territorial behaviour is exhibited in the wild. Movements are unhurried, although they can move quickly and climb easily using their sharp claws. They are poor swimmers.

Development. Sexually mature at 7-8 weeks, they breed throughout the year, rearing up to 11 litters of normally 5-8 young per year. Females mate soon after giving birth, the embryo remaining dormant for up to 18 days if she is lactating. Pregnancy lasts 19-20 days, infants open their eyes at 12 days and are weaned at 18 days.

Food. Seeds, fruits, fungi, insects and household scraps.

Habitat. Most habitats, from deserts to wetter coastal areas.

Status. Common and widespread with occasional population explosions.

Notomys mitchellii MITCHELL'S HOPPING-MOUSE

Distinguished by its long hindlegs and bipedal hopping gait, Mitchell's Hopping-mouse is fawn to dark grey above, often grizzled, and grey-white below. A wide tract of shiny white hairs runs from the throat to chest. The tail is brown or grey above and lighter below with a brush of dark hairs at the tip. The ears are long and oval-shaped with sparse brown hairs outside. Like other rodents they have one pair of upper and lower gnawing incisor teeth and three pairs of molars on each side of the jaw.

Size. Head-body: 100-125 mm. Tail: 140-155 mm. **Weight:** 40-60 g.

Behaviour. Active at night, they shelter during the day in deep burrows around 1.5 m below ground, with several vertical shafts connected to a broad horizontal tunnel 100-150 mm diameter, leading to a nest chamber lined with grass or shredded vegetable matter. Groups of non-breeding adults build adjacent burrow systems up to 150 m apart, with up to 8 adults sharing a burrow to reduce evaporative water loss. Their hopping gait requires less energy than quadrupedal motion at high speeds.

Development. Sexually mature at about 3 months, they probably breed throughout the year in favourable conditions, rearing litters of normally 3-4 young. Pregnancy lasts 34-40 days. Young cling tightly to the mother's teats and are dragged behind her when she moves. They are well-furred at 7 days, their eyes open at 20 days, and are weaned at 30-35 days, living for up to 5 years in captivity.

Food. Seeds, leaves, roots, insects.

Habitat. Semi-arid mallee woodlands, heathlands and shrublands.

Status. Common, widespread.

Mus musculus

Notomys mitchellii

Notomys cervinus

FAWN HOPPING-MOUSE

Found in the arid gibber plains of central Australia, the Fawn Hopping-mouse is a placental mammal with long hindlegs, a distinctive bipedal hopping gait and a long tufted tail. The fur is pale pinkish-fawn to grey above and white below. Males have a naked, raised, flat glandular area on the chest, often stained by orange-yellow secretions in sexually active animals. The ears are long, rounded and sparsely-haired. Like other rodents they have one pair of upper and lower gnawing incisor teeth and three pairs of molars on each side of the jaw.

Size. Head-body: 95-120 mm. Tail: 105-160 mm. **Weight:** 30-50 g.

Behaviour. Active at night, they shelter during the day in simple, humid burrows dug into hard clay or stony soil to 300 mm deep, with 1-3 entrances, shared with up to six other individuals. They live in family groups utilising wide areas and are more aggressive than other hopping-mice, avoiding sandy areas occupied by the rare Dusky Hopping-mouse, *N. fuscus*.

Development. Sexually mature at about 6 months, they are opportunistic breeders, probably reproducing after periods of good rainfall, rearing litters of normally three young. Pregnancy lasts 38-43 days (prolonged by up to 11 days if suckling). Newborn cling to the mother's teats and are dragged around by her if disturbed. Young are well-furred at birth, have their eyes open at about 21 days, and are weaned at 4 weeks.

Food. Seeds, green plant matter and some insects. They will drink salty water and can survive without drinking if necessary.

Habitat. Gibber plains, tussock grasslands and low shrublands with hard clay and stony soils.

Status. Common, widespread.

Notomys alexis

SPINIFEX HOPPING-MOUSE

With its long hindlegs, bipedal hopping gait and long tufted tail, the Spinifex Hopping-mouse is a small distinctive placental mammal of the arid zone. The short fur is light brown to chestnut above and grey-white below. Both sexes have a small throat pouch of unknown function. All males and some females have a naked glandular area on the chest whose secretions may be involved in scent-marking. The ears are long, rounded and sparsely-haired. Like other rodents they have one pair of upper and lower gnawing incisor teeth and three pairs of molars on each side of the jaw.

Size. Head-body: 90-115 mm. Tail: 115-150 mm. **Weight:** 30-50 g.

Behaviour. Active at night, they shelter during the day in deep humid burrows to 1 m below ground, with several vertical shafts connected to a broad horizontal tunnel, leading to a nest chamber lined with grass or shredded vegetable matter. Ten adults may share a burrow, plugging the entrance with sand to reduce evaporative water loss. Runways link adjacent burrow systems used by a social group that cooperates in digging, rearing young and rejecting strangers.

Development. Sexually mature at about 8 weeks, they reproduce after periods of good rainfall, rearing litters of normally 3-4 young. Pregnancy lasts 32-34 days (40 days if suckling four or more young). Young have their eyes open at about 20 days, and are weaned at 4 weeks, living for up to 4 years in captivity.

Food. Seeds, leaves, roots, insects. They can survive without drinking.

Habitat. Arid spinifex and tussock grasslands, woodlands, shrublands and desert sand dunes.

Status. Common, widespread, with marked population fluctuations.

Notomys cervinus

Notomys alexis

Delphinus delphis

COMMON DOLPHIN

Commonly seen in Australian coastal waters, this torpedo-shaped
marine mammal is dark grey to purple black above and cream
to white below with a distinctive hourglass pattern on
the sides. The tips of the snout, lower jaw and lips are
purplish-black. The eyes have black patches around
them. They have a long slender beak, a slender sickle-
shaped dorsal fin, thin tapering flippers and thin tail
flukes with a slight notch in the edge. The jaws have
40-58 pairs of small teeth.
Size. Length: 1.7-2.4 m. **Weight**: 75-136 kg.
Behaviour. Highly sociable, friendly and playful, they congregate
in herds of up to 3,000 or more, following the movements of schools of migrating
fish. Small feeding groups scatter in the late afternoons to feed on organisms rising
to the surface, returning to the herd to rest or play. They can dive to 280 m and
remain submerged for 8 minutes or more, and are often seen playing in the bow
waves of ships. They communicate over long distances using various pulsed sounds
including squawks, squeaks, yaps and shrill whistles, and use high-pitched sounds
to echolocate in dark and murky waters.
Development. Sexually mature at 3-4 years, they mate in spring and autumn at 1-3
year intervals. A single calf, 760-860 mm long, is born 10-11 months later and is
suckled by the mother for 1-3 years.
Food. Migratory fish including herrings, anchovies and sardines; squid.
Habitat. Warm temperate, sub-tropical and tropical coastal waters.
Status. Common.

Tursiops truncatus

BOTTLENOSE DOLPHIN

A coastal, torpedo-shaped marine mammal, the Bottlenose Dolphin is
dark or light grey above grading to light grey on the flanks,
and white or pink below with a blue-grey band from the
base of the beak to each eye. The head is robust with a
relatively short beak with 18-26 pairs of teeth in each
jaw. The lower jaw extends beyond the upper jaw and
curves up slightly. The flippers are pointed, the dorsal
fin is sickle-shaped and the tail flukes are thin with
rounded tips and a notched edge.
Size. Length: 2.3-4 m. **Weight**: 150-650 kg.
Behaviour. Very friendly and playful, they usually swim close to
shore in pods of about 12, forming part of a herd of several hundred animals. Herds
have home ranges of around 85 square kilometres, individual home ranges vary
from 15 to 40 square kilometres according to age and sex. They will chase off and
sometimes kill shark predators. An adult may care for the infant of another dolphin
while the mother feeds. They rise to breathe every 15-20 seconds and can remain
submerged for several minutes, particularly when surf-riding. They communicate
over long distances using various pulsed sounds including squawks, squeaks, yaps
and shrill whistles, and use high-pitched sounds to echolocate in dark and murky
waters. Females whistle almost continually for several days after giving birth to
give an acoustic imprint to their young.
Development. Males are sexually mature at 10-12 years, females at 5-12 years,
living to 35 years or more. Females may produce 8 offspring during their lives at
2-3 year intervals. Calves are born from February to May and September to
November, 12 months after mating. They are 0.9-1.3 m long and suckle for 12-18
months.
Food. Small fish, eels, catfish, mullett and squid.
Habitat. Warm temperate, sub-tropical and tropical coastal waters.
Status. Common.

Delphinus delphis

Tursiops truncatus

Neophoca cinerea

AUSTRALIAN SEA-LION

The only sea-lion seal endemic to Australia, this marine mammal
has a bulky, streamlined body with a blunt snout and a dog-
like head with long whiskers and a very small, rolled
external ear. Adult males are a rich chocolate brown to
blackish with a long mane of white hair over the neck.
Adult females and young are silver-grey to fawn above
and yellow to cream below. They have flippers instead
of forelimbs. The hindlegs are webbed and face the rear.
Size. Length: males 1.85-2.35 m; females 1.3-1.8 m.
Weight: males to 300 kg; females to 80 kg.
Behaviour. Active by day, they rest, moult and breed on land, with
a quadrupedal walk or a fast gallop, sometimes climbing cliffs. They are strong
swimmers mainly using the foreflippers, diving, leaping out of the water and
surfing onto beaches. Most remain within 300 km of their breeding grounds, resting
on sandy beaches and breeding on rocky shores. Pregnant females come ashore
about 3 days before giving birth. Dominant males establish and aggressively defend
a territory into which they heard females, fighting and threatening other males with
loud growls, barks and roars. Females give birth in rocky crevices and gullies.
Development. They breed at about 18 month intervals, giving birth from October
to January or earlier in mild conditions. Females mate 4-9 days after the birth of a
single pup, the embryo remaining dormant for about 4 months, and taking another
14-15 months to develop. Newborn are 600-700 mm long and weigh 6-8 kg. They
have thick soft fur, moult at 2 months, swim at 3 months and suckle for up to 1
year. The mother stays with the pup for 2 weeks then leaves it in a sheltered place
while she feeds at sea, returning every 2 days or so.
Food. Squid, crayfish, fish, cephalopods and penguins.
Habitat. Cool temperate coastal waters, sandy and rocky coastlines.
Status. Sparse.

Dugong dugon

DUGONG

A herbivorous aquatic mammal, the Dugong has a bulky, streamlined
body, grey to bronze above and lighter below with fine
scattered hairs; older animals have large white patches.
They lack hindlimbs, have paddle-like forelimbs and a
horizontal tail-fluke. The head is broad and flat with
nostrils on the top which close when diving, small eyes,
small ear-openings on each side, a large mouth opening
below the head, and short bristles on the muzzle. Males
have a pair of protruding, tusk-like upper incisors.
Size. Length: 2.5-3.3 m. **Weight:** 250-450 kg.
Behaviour. Dugongs spend their lives in the water alone or in herds
of up to several hundred, feeding close to the shore during daylight, commonly
moving 25 km daily. They dive repeatedly for food, staying up to 8.5 minutes
underwater (average 76 seconds). Powerful swimmers, they can move at 22 kph
with up-and-down strokes of the tail flukes, using the flippers to direct and stop
their motion. Active and alert, they form herds of several hundred with no evidence
of large-scale migration. Females give birth in shallow water to avoid sharks. They
have good vision and hearing and utter whistling and chirping sounds.
Development. Sexually mature at 9-15 years, they mate from May to November at
3-6 year intervals, giving birth to a single young 12-14 months later. Females have
two teats in the armpits and males have internal testes. Calves weigh 20-35 kg, are
1-1.25 m long and ride on the mother's back when not suckling, staying with her
for about 2 years. They have a lifespan of up to 73 years.
Food. Seagrasses, supplemented with algae.
Habitat. Shallow tropical coastal waters and estuaries.
Status. Sparse to common. Also in the Indian Ocean, where it is rare.

Neophoca cinerea

Dugong dugon

Arctocephalus forsteri

NEW ZEALAND FUR-SEAL

A streamlined marine mammal with a dog-like head, pointed snout with long whiskers and a small, rolled external ear, this species is dark grey-brown above and lighter below. Bulls have a massive neck and thick mane of coarse hair. Newborn are black and moult at 2 months to become silver-grey. They have strong flippers and webbed hindlegs facing the rear.
Size. Length: males 1.5-2.5 m; females 1.3-1.5 m.
Weight: males 120-200 kg; females 40-70 kg.
Behaviour. They rest, moult and breed on land, moving with a slow shuffling walk, and swim with up-and-down strokes of the webbed hindlimbs. Breeding colonies of up to 1,300 form from October to December when bulls join the cows and juveniles on sheltered, boulder-strewn beaches. The most powerful bulls establish harems of usually six cows in their territories, defended by posturing, guttural barking or fighting savagely if necessary. Bulls leave in late January for their hauling grounds on rocky beaches.
Development. Sexually mature at 4-5 years, males only breed when strong enough to defend a territory at about 10 years of age. Females mate 8 days after giving birth. The embryo remains dormant for some 4 months and takes another 8 months to develop. Newborn are about 550 mm long and weigh some 4 kg. The mother goes to sea to feed 10 days later, returning after 3-5 days to suckle for 2-4 days before leaving again to feed. Pups congregate in pods and are suckled for about 12 months.
Food. Squid, fish, octopus, rock lobster, crab and some penguins.
Habitat. Cool temperate coastal waters, rocky beaches and offshore islands.
Status. Sparse. Common in New Zealand.

Arctocephalus pusillus

AUSTRALIAN FUR-SEAL

The largest and most abundant seal in Australia, this streamlined marine mammal has a dog-like head with long whiskers and a small, rolled external ear. Bulls are dark grey-brown with a mane of long coarse hair. Cows are silver-grey with a creamy-yellow throat and chest and a chocolate-brown abdomen. Pups are dark brown above, yellowish below and moult at 3 months. The forelimbs are flippers and the webbed hindlegs face the rear.
Size. Length: males 2-2.3 m; females 1.2-1.7 m.
Weight: males 218-360 kg; females 36-113 kg.
Behaviour. They rest, moult and breed on land, moving with a slow shuffling walk or a fast gallop, and swim with up-and-down strokes of the webbed hindlimbs. They remain close to their breeding grounds which are usually occupied by females and juveniles. Bulls arrive to breed in late October and the most powerful reoccupy their territories of some 60 square metres, defended by roaring, barking, aggressive postures or fighting off intruding bulls. Cows wander freely and bachelor males congregate on the periphery. Males disperse to feed at sea in January. They have good underwater vision, poor vision on land, and may use echo-location in the water.
Development. Sexually mature at 4-5 years, males only breed when territorial at about 12 years, until defeated 3-6 years later. Females mate 5-7 days after giving birth. The embryo remains dormant for some 3 months and takes another 9 months to develop. Newborn are 600-700 mm long and weigh 4-13 kg. Pups congregate in pods. Females go to sea after mating and return weekly to suckle their pups for 8 months, when they accompany her until weaned by 12 months.
Food. Squid, fish, octopus and rock lobsters. They can dive to 130 m.
Habitat. Cool temperate coastal waters, rocky coastlines.
Status. Sparse. Common in New Zealand.

Arctocephalus forsteri

Arctocephalus pusillus

Hydrurga leptonyx

LEOPARD SEAL

A summer inhabitant of the outer fringes of the Antarctic pack-ice, this streamlined marine mammal moves into Australian coastal waters in winter. The head is reptilian-like with wide gaping jaws and a narrow neck. The long slim body is dark grey above and lighter below with grey or black spots on the sides and throat. Juveniles have a dark stripe on the back and dark spots below. They lack an external ear and have distinctive three-pronged cheek teeth. The forelimbs are flippers, the webbed hindlegs are turned backwards and act as tail flukes for underwater propulsion.

Size. Length: males to 3 m; females to 3.6 m. **Weight:** males to 270 kg; females to 450 kg.

Behaviour. They rest, moult and breed on land, moving caterpillar-like, heaving with the whole body, and swim fast with up-and-down strokes of the webbed hindlimbs. They are solitary and aggressive. Adults live and breed in summer on the outer fringes of the pack-ice and range north in winter. Juveniles disperse widely and poor specimens are sometimes stranded from August to October along the Australian coast. Vocalisations include a throaty alarm call, gurgles, grunts, chirps and whistles.

Development. Females are sexually mature at 2-7 years, males at 3-6 years. They mate from November to March after weaning their young. The embryo remains dormant for some 3 months and takes another 7-8 months to develop. A single pup is born from September to January and is suckled for about 4 weeks.

Food. Krill, fish, cephalopods, penguins, the young of other seals and carrion. They toss penguins around biting off the flesh and leaving the skin.

Habitat. Antarctic and subantarctic seas.

Status. Common. Regular visitors to southern and southeastern Australia.

Megaptera novaeangliae

HUMPBACK WHALE

A massive marine mammal, the Humpback Whale breeds in winter in sub-tropical and tropical Australian coastal waters. The back and sides are grey-black, the belly and throat are usually black and white. The body is stocky with a humpback and long flippers (to 16 m) bearing knobs on the trailing edges. The dorsal fin varies from a small protuberance to a sickle-shaped fin. The head is broad and round, flattened above with barnacle-encrusted knobs on the jaw and 270-400 short baleen plates (used to sieve food from the water) on each side of the upper jaw.

Size. Length: 11-15 m. **Weight:** to about 65 tonnes.

Behaviour. They migrate in winter from feeding grounds in the polar seas to subtropical and tropical breeding areas off the east and west coasts of Australia and other parts of the world. Males advertise their arrival by singing a similar song comprising patterns of cries, yups and chirps, lasting 6-35 minutes, repeated day and night and changing each year. Males congregate around females and often fight to determine which will mate with and/or accompany a particular female. Spectacular jumpers, they will leap out of the water and roll in mid-air. They swim at 4-10 kph (up to 20 kph), surfacing for 3-6 minutes between dives lasting up to 30 minutes, and can echo-locate in dark and murky waters.

Development. Sexually mature at 4-5 years, they live to 30 years or more, mating every 2-3 years. A single young about 4.3 m long is born 11.5 months after mating, is weaned at 7 months, and stays with the mother for 2-3 years.

Food. Krill and small schooling fish, rounded up by blowing a curtain of bubbles around them and lunging into the school with the mouth open.

Habitat. Coastal waters.

Status. Scattered. Regular winter visitors to eastern and western Australia.

Hydrurga leptonyx

Megaptera novaeangliae

Canis familiaris dingo

Introduced to Australia more than 3,000 years ago, the Dingo has colonised all of the mainland. A carnivorous placental mammal, it has long been regarded as a pest, preying on sheep and other domestic livestock. An unsuccessful attempt was made to exclude the Dingo from grazing areas in southern and eastern Australia by erecting the world's longest fence across the Continent. Modern control programmes rely on poisoning, shooting, trapping and local exclusion fencing.

Members of the same species, Dingos interbreed freely with domestic dogs, and wild populations often include many hybrids. The Dingo is typically ginger to sandy-brown with white points, some animals are black with sandy-brown markings. The ears are held erect, the snout is narrower than the domestic dog, the canine teeth are larger and more slender. They have a bushy tail with a scent gland at the base. The legs are slender with five toes on the forefeet and four on the hindfeet. The claws are straight and non-retractable.

Size. Head-body: 860-980 m. Tail: 260-380 mm. **Weight:** 9.5-19.5 kg.

Behaviour. Active mainly at night, they shelter during the heat of the day in a cave or shady spot. Females rear their young in a den in a cave, hollow log or in an excavated rabbit warren, usually within 3 km of water. They are intelligent and secretive animals and are often solitary, foraging alone for small game. They cooperate to hunt larger game such as kangaroos and cattle, forming packs with a dominant male and female and four or five subordinates (usually offspring of previous matings between the dominant pair). They rarely fight, hierarchies are maintained by ritualised postures. The pack is integrated and distinguished from other groups by scent-marking.

They are not territorial, although they usually remain in a well-defined home range which varies in size according to the terrain and abundance of prey, and may be some 20 km across.

Loose short term associations are formed during the breeding season. Non-breeding yearlings often help the parents to rear their young, standing guard and coaching them in hunting techniques.

Dingos are not particularly vocal. They howl to keep contact with others when hunting, to avoid strangers and to attract mates during the breeding season. A howl-bark is used as an alarm signal.

Development. Sexually mature at 9-12 months, they breed once a year, mating from April to June and giving birth to 4-5 pups 63 days after mating. Newborn are blind and well-furred, and are mobile by about 4 weeks. They are weaned at 2 months and remain in the den for another month. If food is scarce they are moved to another den, and may change den sites frequently. The mother regurgitates water and provides food for her pups until they are about 4 months old, when they are capable of hunting themselves. Juveniles often follow their parents until about 12 months old.

Food. An opportunistic predator, mammals are their most important food source, supplemented by reptiles, birds and even insects. Rodents and rabbits are the most common prey in central Australia, and macropods constitute the major part of the diet in southeastern Australia. Domestic livestock is taken, and sheep losses may be large at certain times of the year. They are able to survive for long periods without drinking, obtaining sufficient water from their prey.

Habitat. Most habitats including arid and semi-arid areas with access to drinking water. In southeastern Australia they prefer the margins of forests bordering on heathlands and grasslands.

Status. Common and widespread.

Canis familiaris dingo

BAT STRUCTURE

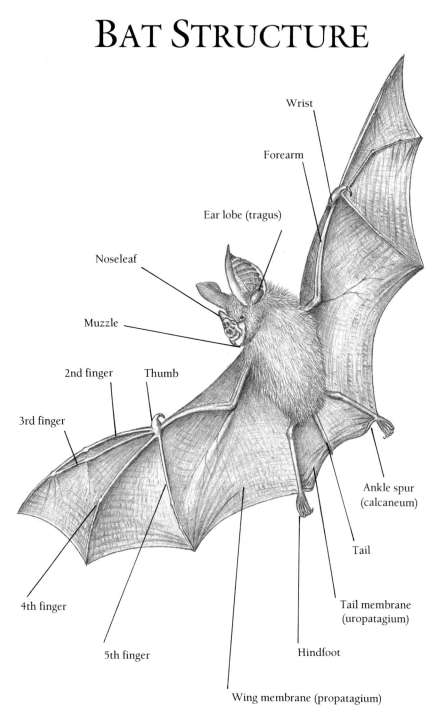

Wrist

Forearm

Ear lobe (tragus)

Noseleaf

Muzzle

2nd finger

Thumb

3rd finger

Ankle spur
(calcaneum)

4th finger

Tail

5th finger

Tail membrane
(uropatagium)

Hindfoot

Wing membrane (propatagium)

FURTHER READING

Archer, M. (ed), 1982. *Carnivorous Marsupials*. Royal Zoological Society of NSW.

Baker, A.N., 1983. *Whales and Dolphins of New Zealand and Australia*. Victoria University Press, Wellington.

Bureau of Flora and Fauna, 1987. *Fauna of Australia*. Australian Government Printing Service, Canberra.

Bureau of Flora and Fauna, 1988. *Zoological Catalogue of Australia. Mammalia* Australian Government Printing Service, Canberra.

Covacevich, J.E. and Easton, A., 1974. *Rats and Mice in Queensland*. Queensland Museum, Brisbane.

Cronin. L. (ed), 1987. *Koala*. Reed Books, Sydney.

Evans, P.G.H., 1987. *The Natural History of Whales and Dolphins*. Helm, London.

Flannery, T.F., 1990. *Australia's Vanishing Mammals*. R.D. Press, Sydney.

Grant, T.R., 1984. *The Platypus*. University of NSW Press, Sydney.

Griffiths, M., 1978. *The Biology of the Monotremes*. Academic Press, New York.

Grigg, G.C., Jarman, P. and Hume, I.D., 1989. *Kangaroos, Wallabies and Rat Kangaroos*. Surrey Beatty and Sons, Sydney.

Hall, L.S. and Richards, G.C., 1979. *Bats of Eastern Australia*. Queensland Museum, Brisbane.

King, J.E., 1983. *Seals of the World*. University of Queensland Press, London.

Ride, W.D.L., 1970. *A Guide to the Native Mammals of Australia*. Oxford University Press, Melbourne.

Smith, A. and Hume, I.D., 1984. *Possums and Gliders*. Surrey Beatty and Sons, Sydney.

Stonehouse, B. and Gilmore, D., 1977. *The Biology of Marsupials*. University Park Press, Baltimore.

Strahan, R., 1983. *The Australian Museum Complete Book of Australian Mammals*. Angus and Robertson, Sydney.

Strahan, R., 1987. *What Mammal is That?* Angus and Robertson, Sydney.

Thornback, J., and Jenkins, M., 1982. *The IUCN Mammal Red Data Book*. IUCN, Switzerland.

Tyndale-Biscoe, C.H., 1973. *Life of Marsupials*. Arnold, London.

Tyndale-Biscoe, C.H. and Renfree, M.B., 1987. *Reproductive Physiology of Marsupials*. Cambridge University Press, Cambridge.

Watts, C.H.S. and Aslin, H.J., 1981. *The Rodents of Australia*. Angus and Robertson, Sydney.

ACKNOWLEDGEMENTS

Without the dedication of the many hundreds of researchers who have painstakingly studied the biology of the Australian mammals, and whose work I have freely drawn upon, this would be a very slim volume. A number of people gave much of their time and expertise in the preparation of this book, and I would like to express my special thanks to the staff of the Australian Museum; in particular to Linda Gibson, who facilitated access to the museum's collection of mammals and made constructive criticism of the illustrations; to Tim Flannery, who checked the distribution maps; to Tish Ennis; and to the staff of the library who put in a great deal of legwork on my behalf. Many thanks to Ray Williams who gave unstintingly of his time and knowledge, and was of immeasurable help with reference material. Thanks to Steven Waterhouse, a keen young naturalist, who sought out illustrative reference works with unbounded enthusiasm, and to Colin Gudgeon who also helped with reference material. Thanks to the staff of Macquarie University Fauna Park; the staff of Featherdale Wildlife Park; and the staff of Koala Park. Thanks also to Jonathan Clemens who proof-read the manuscript and offered much constructive advice.

INDEX

SCIENTIFIC NAMES

INDEX

COMMON NAMES